She and You and Me

and Me

Finding Ourselves
in the Bible

Margaret Passenger

H AND M
PUBLISHING

Joan—

Continued blessings
on your way.

Matthew 7:7

Pastor Margaret

She and You and Me
Finding Ourselves in the Bible

Printed in Michigan
United States of America

First Printing

Published in the United States of America
H and M Publishing, Monroe, MI 48162

ISBN 978-0-9898183-0-8

Home Editor and Formatter: Henry Passenger
Professional Editor: Kathy Steffen
Cover Designer: LindaVilas-Helton
Printed by Color House Graphics, Inc.

Permissions

In memory of
Aunt Doris,
who long ago told me
I should write

"What would happen
if one woman
told the truth about her life?
The world would split open."
— *Muriel Rukeyser* (1913-1980)

"For we cannot help speaking
about what we have seen
and heard."
— *Acts 4:20, NIV*

For I cannot help writing
about what I have learned
and lived.
— *Acts 4:20, paraphrased*

She and You and Me

Contents

Introduction

The purpose of this book is to encourage women to find themselves in the Bible. Men could find themselves there too, but that would be another book, perhaps for a man to write. The Bible isn't a bunch of dusty old stories to store on a shelf. It may have been written centuries ago, but it contains all a person could want. If you're looking for love, it's there. If you're looking for murder, it's there too. Transfiguration? Yes. Incest? Yes. The good, the bad, the ugly. The raw and the sublime.

Biblical writers were not afraid to tell it true. And because Biblical truth is so powerful, I believe we are meant to find ourselves in the Bible's pages, to see ourselves in its stories. We are meant to be able to say, "I am like that person"; "I know that character"; "That psalm says exactly what's in my heart."

This book also tells my story, revealing my good, my bad, my ugly, my joys, my sorrows, my struggles and successes. It contains portraits and snapshots of people who have been important in my life. It traces my evolution as a human being. I am not what I was; I am not what I will be.

In my first career, I taught high school English. My second career was journalism – newspaper copy editing. My third, from which I retired, was ministry in The United Methodist Church. I hope my background in ministry does not make me "different" or "distant" in your eyes. Pastors are just like everyone else. We may serve in a special niche of ministry, but all God's children have God-given gifts and graces and are called to be in ministry to each other. Each of us has a special voice someone needs to hear. We all have stories to share, and we all are called to be witnesses to God's mercy and grace.

Scores of women are mentioned in the Bible. Some of them are included here – Abigail, Miriam, Dorcas, Lois, and Lydia, to name five. Each is an example of courage and faith.

Like these women, you and I are called to courage and faith. That is another message of this book. It is easier to talk about being courageous than to act it, I know, but no matter our age, if we sense God speaking to us or the Holy Spirit nudging us to begin a new career or set out in a new direction, we need to take the leap and say yes.

If nerves threaten to "undo us," we can think of Jesus' mother, Mary. She was so "greatly troubled" at the angel's birth announcement she asked, "How will this be, since I am a virgin?" We can think of Jael, the Old Testament heroine who conquered an enemy commander. Did she have second thoughts before she did the deed? We can think of Ruth and Naomi, who left Moab and trudged the road back to Judah – two widows alone, as far as we know, walking the dust of a desert. Did they even own enough provisions to load on the back of a donkey?

These women's stories are told in this book. Each of them may have been frightened, but each was a daughter of God nonetheless. God's hand upheld them. And when you and I walk with God, God's hand upholds us too. It is a divine guarantee. So if you're 35, 45, 55, late 60s like me – or even 91 – say yes. Be brave. Reach for new life.

Have you seen the billboard of the 95-year-old college graduate? Robed in traditional black, her white hair fluffed out under her cap, she is "Possibility Realized." Her pride is evident. Her smile says it all.

My husband and I have said many times as our lives have unfolded together, "The adventure continues." Life is full of challenges, but it is a glorious and God-blessed adventure if we choose to consider it so. So come along on the adventure of this book. May you see yourself in its pages and find yourself in the Bible.

To that end and to facilitate use of the book for individual or group exploration, refer to the Users' Guides in the appendix.

For you created my inmost being;
you knit me together in my mothers's womb.
Psalm 139:13, NIV

Mary, Mother of Jesus
Giving Birth to the Holy

Perhaps you've heard the song *"We Are Standing on Holy Ground."* I feel like I'm writing on holy ground when I mention Mary. She is sanctified, venerated, pure. She bears names that signify status – Mother of God, Madonna, Virgin, Our Lady, Blessed Mother, Queen of Heaven.

How do I properly and respectfully write about Mary? Do I dare to see myself in her? Am I being sacrilegious? Can I aspire to be anything like her? Is she so holy I cannot reach her?

The answers are yes and no. No, I cannot reach her because her holiness was on the highest of planes, surpassed only by Jesus. But yes, I can aspire to be like her because she was a human being, a woman on this earth. She was married, gave birth, and watched a child die. She asked questions, pondered things in her heart, and made a request of her son. One time she even chastised him when she and her husband found him at the temple – she was a mother scolding her son. So yes, I am like her in some ways. You are like her too.

Go back to pre-Bethlehem circa the year 4 B.C. You're expecting a baby and you find you must travel to fulfill the mandate of a census. You cannot walk the distance. Your husband helps you onto a donkey, and you bounce and sway to its rhythms. You feel the time grow short. The baby will come soon. Will you reach Bethlehem in time?

When you arrive, there is no suitable place to give birth. Every hotel room is taken and a hospital doesn't exist. There isn't even a midwife. Finally, an innkeeper allows you and your husband to use the stable out back. You bear your baby, swaddle him, smile down at him, protect him. You cuddle the most precious of gifts. Overwhelming love washes over you, love for your baby and for the Lord of the Universe, who chose you to mother His son.

It is the Christmas story, narrated by Matthew (*Chapter 1:18-25*) and by Luke (*Chapter 2:1-20*).

My daughter, Marcia, came into the world at 11:36 p.m. February 2, 1971. I didn't get to hold her until the next morning. She'd taken her time in arriving. Labor lasted 40 hours. When the nurse put her in my arms, wrapped in traditional pink, I hardly dared unfold the blanket to take a close-up look. She was sleeping, and I didn't want to wake her. With awe, I found tiny nails on tiny fingers and even tinier nails on tiny toes. Soft reddish-blonde hair crowned her head. I just looked and looked at my beautiful baby. The pain of the night before was gone, and it *was*, truly, love at first sight.

I wondered what kind of a mother I would be. Could I do justice to the greatest job with which a woman is entrusted? I doubted myself. Fortunately, a friend "held my hand" during those early days at home, and Marcia's sweet nature made motherhood not a job but a privilege.

Years later I held my grandson, Thomas (Henry's daughter's son), when he was two hours old, even newer than Marcia had been when I first held her. Instant love coursed through me again. And with him, there was no pain. I was Grandma; his mother had endured the Caesarian. I cradled that precious sleeping boy, watching him breathe and giving grateful thanks for the miracle of life.

Then I handed him to Henry, standing near me in Penny's room. Grandpa stands 6'3" and tops 250 on the scale. He did not cradle Thomas to his chest but supported him on his hands, standing straight in silence and peering into that new face. What went through his mind? Hopes and fears? Dreams and destinies?

I didn't ask, and Henry never told me. I just kept my eyes on him holding his brand-new grandson. And I marveled, as I always do, at a big man carrying a baby. Finally he handed Thomas back to me, and I returned him to his mother.

The newborn and his family came home from the hospital to our house and stayed with us for two weeks. Penny and nine-year-old Patrick needed more time to get their apartment ready to be a home to the new baby. Grandpa helped them, and, while they were gone, I had a chance to grand-mother Thomas for hours uninterrupted. One day, especially, I remember sitting with my week-old grandson in my platform rocker, cuddling him, dozing with him and, every few hours, warming up two-ounce bottles. I had never seen such tiny bottles before. There weren't any that small that I knew of 35 years earlier when Marcia was born.

Holding Thomas, singing softly at

times, caring for his needs, I had no doubt I was doing what I was meant to do that day. The words to "Silent Night" rang very true – "Sleep in heavenly peace. Sleep in heavenly peace."

My nephew, Michael, was two months old the first time I saw him and held him. His mother, my sister, was wheeling him down a long walkway in Stapleton Airport in Denver. Michael was hard to miss. His bright orange Denver Broncos sweatsuit stood out, even from a long way off, and the nearer we got to each other, the more I could tell there was something unusual about  this baby. His head seemed to sit on his shoulders. I called him Mr. No Neck. He was one of those babies who simply had to "grow into" his neck.

It didn't take too long. After maturing through the toddler stage, the handsome little guy won a trophy as a two-year-old Mr. Denver.

One of the privileges of pastoring is baptizing, especially babies. The youngest for whom I performed that sacrament was three weeks old. Her parents carried her forward in a traditional white baptismal gown, and when they placed that tiny girl in my arms, the people in the front pew heard me gasp. I hadn't held an infant that small in a long time, and I was looking down at the face of perfection. Tears came to my eyes, and I had to compose myself before continuing the liturgy.

Baby Chloe slept through the whole thing, not even awakening when I moistened her head with water from the River Jordan. She did not stir as I intoned the ancient words of "I baptize you in the name of the Father, and of the Son, and of the Holy Spirit." She did not know we welcomed her into our congregation of the family of God, and she rested quietly in her mother's arms as we sang *"Child of Blessing, Child of Promise"* to encourage and love her on her way.

Thank you, loving God, for creating women to be child bearers and giving us the opportunity to be mothers.

QUESTIONS FOR LIFE:

1. Are you a mother? What was your experience(s) of giving birth? What did you feel and think when you first saw your baby? What fears, hopes and dreams did you have?

2. Do you resonate with Mary? Can you see yourself at all like her, cuddling your newborn, perhaps singing softly and smiling?

3. What is your opinion about this statement? "Your child ultimately belongs to God and you are entrusted as the caretaker."

4. How do you react to seeing a man holding or carrying a young baby?

5. Are you an adoptive mother or an aunt? Describe the day the new little person came into your life.

6. Are you a grandmother? What are your first memories of meeting a new grandchild?

Let us not become conceited,
*   provoking and envying each other.*
*   Galatians 5:26, NIV*

Martha and Mary
The Sisters

Were they sibling rivals? The Bible doesn't say, but it might seem that way in the home-visit story told in the gospel of Luke. Martha wanted Mary to help her prepare the house for Jesus. But when he arrived, instead of offering assistance, Mary sat at his feet and listened to him talk. Martha asked Jesus to intervene. Instead, he told her that Mary had chosen "what is better, and it will not be taken away from her."   *Luke 10:42, NIV*

        Was Jesus hard on Martha? I've always thought so because she opened her home to him as a hostess and most likely fed him. Entertaining takes preparation, and extra help may be appreciated. Martha might have been distracted with her tasks, as Jesus said, but since Mary left her with all the work, no wonder she was upset.

The sisters and their brother, Lazarus, are mentioned several places in the gospels, but this story is found in *Luke 10:38-42*.

My sister and I fit the picture – sibling rivals for sure. Do you know any brothers and sisters who weren't, at least those close in age?

"What a cute little girl," anyone might have said about my two-year-old sister. Her  alert brown eyes took in everything, and an almost-impish smile played on her lips. She wore her hair short and straight and parted in the middle, bangs low on her forehead, styled that way by our mother. My hair was parted in the middle too, but each side sported a bow, sometimes a big one. A childhood photo shows those two big bows sticking up so high no one could miss 'em. Today I look at that picture and see those bows as helicopter rotors ready to whisk me out of sight. In those early childhood days, I was just plain jealous that Becky didn't have to wear bows in her hair.

When Mom and Dad moved from Iowa to Michigan and our Indiana grandparents took care of us, three-year-old Becky came down with chicken pox. One afternoon Grandma laid her on a braided rug in the yard, allowing the sunshine to dry the pox spots. I yanked the rug from under my sister and "caught it" from my grandmother. I deserved the scolding, I know, but Becky *was* getting all the attention.

And then there were clothes – my sizes large, Becky's sizes small. Starting in junior high, she swiped sweaters and skirts without asking and wore them loosely, but I could never fit into anything of hers to be able to "borrow" back.

In school classes, however, the rivalry reversed. "Oh, you're Margie's sister," some of the teachers commented, remembering me from three years before. That hurt, Becky said, and I was sorry to hear it, but obviously I did not know what it felt like to be a second child – a younger sister.

Also in teen years, when tempers flared, fingernails morphed into weapons. (Did you ever use yours that way?) We dug in and held position on each other's forearms, not drawing blood or clawing, but not budging either, enduring pain and grooves in tender skin rather than crying "Uncle." Usually I backed off first, disgusted at myself for giving in.

I never did give in, though, with the Orange Nut Bread. The summer of 1960 when my church youth group was scheduled for a work trip to Wadley, Alabama, we were asked to bring a homemade goodie for everyone to share. I scoured my mother's cookbooks and found a recipe that sounded delicious. I followed the directions to the letter and expected fragrant, fantastic results. Well, fragrancy filled the kitchen air, but the results fell far short of fantastic. The loaf pan "weighed a ton" as I removed it from the oven, and the contents were "hard as a rock." That bread could have served as a jack for the church bus. Not a crumb – if one could have been cracked off – was fit to eat.

Becky razzed the dickens out of me about that bread. My 13-year-old sister was derisive, absolutely convinced I'd made a mistake. I defended myself, of course, but she had me wondering. I'd been so careful, and the results were so unexpected.

Three summers later Becky's youth group was slated for a work trip to New Hampshire. The request was the same. "Please bring a homemade goodie for everyone to share." Remembering my Orange Nut Bread, she decided she'd make it right, prove that I'd been wrong and win the baking battle. So she was careful, too, measuring and sifting and mixing the ingredients as directed. Waiting and watching as her bread baked, I partly wanted her to succeed and partly to fail. She was so sure of herself.

The results? *Her* product was just as hard as mine. *Her* pan felt like lead, and *her* bread could have served as a bus jack too. I felt a bit bad but, more importantly, I felt vindicated.

We finally decided, after "cooking" our arguments, that we'd run into a bad recipe. Rival sisters Margie and Becky pretty much came to a draw on that one.

Still, Martha-Becky Mary-Me was evident early. Mom would dress me first when we were little and sit me in a chair to wait. But if she worked with Becky first and even momentarily turned her back, Becky would scramble down, forcing Mom to look to find her. Different temperaments in different little girls.

And true of us as adult women as well. Becky inherited our mother's love of cooking and giftedness as a hostess. (There must be a gene that passed me by.) For her children's birthdays, she baked sensational cakes. One year, her daughter Elena's dragon wore green "paint" and grinned gleefully, mouth agape. Excited kids stared before digging in. *"See what my mommy made,"* Elena might have bragged to her friends.

For a high school graduation party, Becky carved a peacock from a watermelon, fanning the tail with skewers laced with fruit. Hungry guests took little time making them "fold up" and disappear.

Many Christmases my daughter, Marcia, and I flew to Denver and then in more recent years to Peachtree City, Georgia, where Becky and her family moved in 1988. Their home, set amid the pines, reflected Becky's decorating talent and Charlie's landscaping skill. The stockings *were hung* by the chimney with care, and luminaries lined the driveway on Christmas Eve.

Becky's table shone with stemware, and her centerpiece sparkled in the mirror on which it sat. Becky had cooked ahead of time, and we feasted on goodies galore.

But there are certain things for Christmas dinner that cannot be done in advance. Like turkey gravy. Becky would start it with a roux, add some broth, and when it was simmering, call me to stir. Mary (me) would join Martha (her) in the kitchen for tasting to make sure the seasonings were right.

Whenever I make gravy, I think of Christmas and my sister.

Thank you, dear God, for the relationship called sister. It is truly a bond like none other.

Addendum: For another Biblical look at rivalry between sisters, read the story of Rachel and Leah in Genesis 29:1-35:20.

QUESTIONS FOR LIFE:

1. Are you a Martha? Are you a Mary? Are you some of both?

2. Do you have a sister(s)? Were you, or are you still, rivals?

3. How did you and your sister(s) get along in the past? What about now?

4. Is sibling rivalry inevitable? Can it ever be a good thing? How? Why?

5. Is there any place for rivalry in the family of God? Why or why not?

6. Read the story of Leah and Rachel. What is your reaction?

Praise the Lord...
Praise him for his acts of power...
Praise him with tambourine and dancing...
Let everything that has breath praise the Lord.
Psalm 150, selected verses, NIV

Miriam
Singer/Musician

"*O thou great Jehovah, protect my little baby brother. Help my mother put this basket in a good place so someone will find it quickly. Help it be watertight and float to the right place in this big, wide river, the Nile.*" So the Hebrew girl Miriam might have prayed on the day she helped her mother save a son who would someday lead his people out of Egypt. *Exodus 2:1-10*

And when that day came many years later, Miriam would join Moses in song, praising the God who had parted the waters and was leading the Israelites to the Promised Land. The Old Testament says Miriam "took a tambourine in her hand, and all the women followed her, with tambourines and dancing. Miriam sang to them:

'Sing to the Lord
for he is highly exalted.
The horse and its rider
he has hurled into the sea.' "

Exodus 15:20-21, NIV

"Hi Babe, Hi Babe, whatcha doin' tonight, Babe?"

I sang that little ditty when I was two years old. How did I learn such a song? My mother coached and taught me.

What might she have been thinking, teaching me those words? They could have meant a cool dude was asking a chick for a date! Of course at the age of two, I had no idea what I was singing. But so began a lifelong love of music, a daughter absorbing a passion of her mother's.

My mother started studying piano when she was six, practicing every day at an old black upright that hugged a wall in her home in Gladstone, Michigan, a small town on the Lake Michigan shoreline in the Upper Peninsula. She sang as well as played, in school and in church – sometimes solos, sometimes duets, with a best friend or a cousin.

Mom majored in English and music in college and finished her career in education years later, teaching elementary kids to sing. She directed hundreds of them in musical programs – the kind that bring beams to parents' faces. She had a way; the kids always responded.

When I was a baby, Mom directed a Presbyterian church choir in Galveston, Texas. My father was on the physiology faculty at the University of Texas Medical School at the time. One Saturday night they were invited to a graduate student party, where cool cups of pretty green punch awaited their enjoyment. My mother downed several, not knowing someone had doctored the drink. She couldn't taste the vodka, and the Tipsy Punch took effect. The next morning, wouldn't you know, the choir anthem she directed was "*God Is a Spirit*," and some of those grad guys sat in that choir, nearly grinnin' their heads off.

In our home in East Lansing, Michigan, where we moved when I was six, the spinet piano sat next to a Hammond organ. Mom learned to play the organ, but it was my Uncle Alcott who brought that instrument to life. A naturally gifted musician, he could play almost anything. He and my mother played duets, selections running the gamut from show stoppers to Stephen Foster, Debussy to Brahms, patriotic American tunes to great old hymns of the church. Sometimes we'd all sing along, and our house would be filled with the sound of music. Both Mother and Alcott played and sang with passion.

Mom's friend, Edna, also loved to sing as Mom played. With her wide vocal range, Edna could reach deep and low, almost to baritone level. She sang with full-bodied richness, as if all the power of Odin's Norse handmaidens, the Valkyries, was at her command. When she sang about her native Norway, she was there in her heart, and listening, I saw the jagged mountain peaks and the deep, majestic fjords.

Two Christmases before my mother died, she spent the holiday with my husband,  Henry, and me and my daughter, Marcia. By that time Mom's hair was nearly white, and she wore it short and sassy, flipped up at the ends. A photo shows her in a patterned sweater seated at our piano, arthritic fingers on the keys. She was slowing down at 86, but her eyes were bright. She could still make a piano sing. We enlarged that photo and displayed it at her memorial service two years later.

Like my mother, I began piano lessons at age six. But unlike her, I gave them up.

Recitals petrified me. I was always too frightened to let myself go and lose myself in the music.

I did better with singing. I was a member of Mom's youth choir in our church. I also sang in junior high, and as a high school student added my voice to a large, but not select, group. One day our director switched the soprano and alto sections because the sopranos complained that their part went too low and the altos that theirs ranged too high. Mr. Steiner told us we could do it, stretch our young voices and surprise ourselves. I never would have believed it, but at that time I hit a high G as clear as a bell.

My biggest thrill took place in the chapel at Michigan State University. Our East Lansing High School chamber choir had been invited to sing the choruses in Verdi's *Requiem,* challenging, God-inspired, rich music for high school kids. I stood straight and tall, almost soldier-like, sensing the solemnity of the occasion. I felt sophisticated and very grown up.

If I were asked to name a favorite

piece of music to sing, it would be *"Open My Eyes, That I May See,"* a grand old hymn of the Church. If I were asked to name a favorite composer, it would be Beethoven, without a doubt.

Thank you, great and wondrous God, for the magnificent gift of music.

QUESTIONS FOR LIFE:

1. Have you ever played the tambourine or any other percussion instrument? If so, what are your favorite memories?

2. If you ever took piano or any other kind of instrumental lessons, what memories come to mind? What do you recall about your beginner days or about special performances later on?

3. What is your experience with singing? What are some of your favorite songs?

4. What kind of music inspires you? What would you say if you were writing your own chapter about music?

Therefore, as God's chosen people,
holy and dearly loved,
clothe yourselves with compassion,
kindness, humility, gentleness and patience.
Colossians 3:12, NIV

Dorcas
The Seamstress

Have you ever known anyone who was goodness personified? I believe Dorcas (Tabitha, in Hebrew) could be seen that way.

She lived in the Mediterranean seacoast city of Joppa, a center of commerce and trade, where the townspeople knew her for her good deeds and help to the poor. Sewing robes and other articles of clothing was her trademark. Her skill was so well known that when she died and Simon Peter was called to her bedside, her friends showed him the robes and other clothing Dorcas had put together. Peter prayed and brought Dorcas back to life, an act that "became known all over Joppa, and many people believed in the Lord."   *Acts 9:36-42, NIV*

The doll clothes were beautiful. My mother could have made them herself, but she claimed no confidence working with small sections of cloth. A friend made the outfits for my "walking" doll and my sister's.

Becky and I received those dolls from Santa the Christmas I was nine and she was six. We played with them most of Christmas Day, parading them across the living-room, dressing and undressing them to see how each item fit. I don't remember how many pieces of clothing there were or if pajamas and a robe were included, but I do remember the winter coat. If I had taken my doll outside, she would have been toasty warm and elegant in brown tweed with a matching hat.

Two years before, when I was seven

and Becky was four, we wore dresses Mother *had* made, along with one for herself. The family had gathered to celebrate Grandpa's 75th birthday, and Mom decided that matching mother-daughter dresses would be perfect for the occasion. She chose soft yellow organdy and a pattern with a flared skirt. Our dresses billowed in the soft August breeze. I felt pretty in that dress, posing for a family picture and hearing Mom receive numerous compliments about her handiwork. She'd made good use of her portable Singer sewing machine.

I think the smocking Mom did, however, had to be done by hand. Gathering the material into tiny pleats and spacing them evenly on each bodice took time and precision. I don't remember how many dresses she smocked for Becky or me, but Jane, our cousin, says Aunt Ginny made two dresses for her, a brown one and a white one with bright red smocking, delivered in time for Valentine's Day 1949. Jane says smocked dresses can still be found in specialty shops for little girls. And perhaps smocking is still a skill seamstresses practice at home.

In 1966, for my wedding to Bob, the mother of the bride wore her own creation. Her short-sleeved olive green sheath was fashionable for the time. Why Mom chose that color I don't know, except she liked it, and she never feared being unique. The green extended even to her head, because she had enough material to drape around her pillbox hat, which included a bow sticking up at the top. With matching gloves and heels, she greeted guests in the receiving line as Mrs. Coordination.

When it came my turn to learn to sew, I started with a dish towel. I was in 5th grade, in 4-H. Our assignment of hemming didn't sound too difficult, but I had a hard time folding the material evenly to a quarter-inch. And when I looked at that first seam, it was ocean wavy instead of straight. I don't know how many times I struggled to get it right, and I don't remember ever using that towel to dry any dishes.

Next up? An apron – not like a chef's apron with a bib, but one that tied at the waist. The gathering and fitting and long waistband were new challenges for us ten-year-olds to conquer.

Eventually I got the hang of sewing and enjoyed it. At 15, my gray wool suit with deep red blouse won "Best Clothing Project" at our county fair, and, with matching red hat and heels and white gloves, I modeled it at the Michigan State Fair in Detroit.

I didn't do much sewing as a young

housewife and mother, but one Halloween I decided to make Marcia's costume. She wanted to be a princess. I tried to make her look like one, but my sweet daughter would have been better served if she'd said, *"I want to be Cinderella,"* and I'd bought her a gown from Disney.

A few years later, a friend offered to teach tailoring. She had made several sports coats for her husband. Bob approved the soft beige color I selected. I cut carefully, following Marlene's directions, tackling lapels and pockets and linings. Bob wore his coat for years, and I never made anything better.

Since those days in the 1970s, I've purchased a newer and fancier sewing machine, but I haven't used it for a long time. The bright red thread from the summer of 1998 is still in the bobbin, wound there for a Christmas stocking project.

In August 1998, Henry taught a four-week course in China, helping Chinese teachers learn American customs and idiomatic American English. He couldn't mention anything religious about Christmas, but he and his colleagues could discuss the secular and cultural aspects of the celebration – like red felt stockings. He asked me to make them, and, as the needle whirred, I wondered who the recipients might be, what their lives were like, and whether some of them might ever be able to come to the United States and experience an American Christmas for themselves.

I don't know whether I'll ever get my machine in working order again, now that I'm a grandma with graying hair, but I know my younger years were enriched by the art and craft of sewing.

God of inspiration, thank you for our talents and gifts. Help us use our creativity to enrich one another.

QUESTIONS FOR LIFE:

1. Are you a seamstress? What have you made? What item are you most proud of?

2. How old were you when you first learned to sew? What are some of your early memories?

3. Have you ever sewed, like Dorcas – or knitted or quilted or crocheted or tatted – for your community or for a mission project? What did you make? Describe your efforts and your feelings about what you accomplished. What was it like joining with others in such a project?

Don't be in any rush to become a teacher,
my friends.
Teaching is highly responsible work.
Teachers are held to the strictest standards.
James 3:1, The Message

Priscilla
The Teacher

Apollos didn't have it quite right. He knew the basics, but he wasn't sharing the whole story of Jesus. Priscilla and her husband, Aquila, set him straight. They took him to their home in Ephesus (western Turkey) and filled him in.

Apollos had learned much about Jesus in his native city of Alexandria, in northern Africa, but he "knew only the baptism of John," according to the Book of Acts. He spoke boldly, but he had not received nor did he understand Jesus' baptism with the Holy

Spirit. So Priscilla and Aquila "invited him to their home and explained to him the way of God more adequately." Through team-teaching, they provided Apollos with information he lacked. In turn, he took it and "vigorously refuted the Jews in public debate, proving from the Scriptures that Jesus was the Christ." Together, the three of them served as powerful ambassadors for Christ, ministering in the footsteps of their mentor, Paul, and helping to grow the early Church.

Acts 18:24-28, NIV

At first I didn't want any part of it. Dad was a teacher. Mom was a teacher. Why would I want to be one?

Early on, I leaned toward nursing. But soon I learned I couldn't stand to see a needle poked in an arm. The sight of blood didn't bother me, but hooking up an IV? Not for me. So how could I ever have thought I'd make it in that medical profession?

The change in my career direction

took place my senior year in high school. In English class we studied British literature. The Shakespeare curriculum called for *Macbeth*. One day, without a preamble, Mrs. Sharer began: "Double, double toil and trouble, fire burn, and cauldron bubble," cackling the speech, fire in eyes and fingers spread wide, as if hovering over that boiling pot and seeing the spirits of the dead. All she lacked were the long, sharp fingernails, the cape, and the pointed black hat. Her performance mesmerized me. And even though I didn't like the vocabulary study that accompanied that great literature, the hook was set. From then on I knew I wanted to be an English teacher.

That fall I enrolled at Michigan State, and my love of Shakespeare continued. You might say I was "bard" obsessed since I took three classes, paying far more attention to him than the romantic poets – Byron, Keats and Shelley. I minored in French, and *beaucoup* literature surrounded me in those classes too.

That freshman year, one of my

professors made as much of an impression on me as Mrs. Sharer did. Dr. Frederick Reeve had been an editor for one of the major dictionaries. One day he approached me when I couldn't define a word and said, looking down through bifocals perched on end of nose, "Young lady, don't you *always* use a dictionary when you read?" I answered, "No, sir." "Well, I suggest that from now on, you do." His seriousness and size, as well as his resounding voice, made me feel I'd better pay attention. To this day, if I meet a word I don't know, I feel compelled to look it up.

Somehow, I met the College of Education requirements. The classes bored me – education theory and sociology – and I didn't understand them. But I knew I had to pass them to become certified. Student teaching, thankfully, provided much-needed hands-on experience.

Sarah, a best friend, and I shared a log cabin on the shores of Grand Traverse Bay in the northwestern Lower Peninsula that winter term of 1965 – two "college kids" student teaching at Traverse City High School. I was only four years older than the kids in my classes. When I think back on all the red-mark corrections I scratched on their senior term papers, I cringe. At the time, I thought I was doing my job. I did try to find something commendable in each paper, but overall I lacked wisdom and compassion, and didn't temper criticism with mercy.

By the end of student teaching, I knew I'd be returning to TCHS the next fall. My supervising teacher recommended me, and the Traverse City Public Schools decided to hire me to teach sophomore English – at a salary of $4,300.

If any of you are teachers, you know how difficult the first year of teaching can be. I lived by myself in a four-room apartment and put in three hours of homework every night, grading papers and making lesson plans, striving to stay ahead of my students.

In August 1966, Bob and I married and moved to Clare, in the upper middle of Michigan's Lower Peninsula. Clare High School became home for two years while I taught sophomores again, 15- and 16-year-olds who educated me far more than I taught them.

One young man I simply couldn't motivate to read or to care about spelling. I suggested *Popular Mechanics*, thinking a magazine about cars and gadgets could serve as a catalyst for reading. As for spelling, he said he wouldn't need to know how because he intended to become a business boss whose secretary would do the spelling for him. His attitude set me back a bit, but somehow, with that brassy young man, I could imagine such a scenario taking place.

One more year of full-time teaching followed our years in Clare after Bob and I moved to Monroe, Michigan, in the southeast corner of the state, in 1969. After that, while mothering young Marcia, I taught seven years part-time, still high school English, but in adult education programs administered by two different school districts.

Teaching English was my first career.

God of instruction and love, thank you for faithful teachers and the powerful influence for good they often provide in the lives of their students.

QUESTIONS FOR LIFE:

1. What do you think of Priscilla (and Aquila) as a teacher?

2. Which teacher(s) had the most impact on you? Why? How? Were they the ones who taught you the most?

3. What were the lasting lessons you learned in school?

4. Has the Holy Spirit ever been your teacher? When and how?

5. In what ways have you been a teacher in your life?

6. The Bible mentions false teachers. How can we recognize them?

7. What do you think is the most important quality for a teacher to possess? Why?

"Your servant is in your hands," Abram said.
"Do with her whatever you think best."
Then Sarai mistreated Hagar;
so she fled from her.

Genesis 16:6, NIV

Sarah
Maternal Ruler/Matriarch

Abraham was a man of God. He and God were good buddies. But what kind of a husband was he? Likely he had his hands full with Sarah.

For one thing, she was beautiful, so beautiful that when they lived in Egypt, Abraham (named Abram at the time) told Sarah (Sarai at the time) to lie and tell the Egyptians she was his sister, not his wife. His reasoning? If the Egyptians knew she was his wife, they would kill him. "Say you are my sister, so that I will be treated well for your sake and my life will be spared because of you."   *Genesis 12:13, NIV*

    She did as directed. And things went well for him. Sarai was taken to Pharaoh's palace and "Abram acquired sheep and cattle, male and female donkeys, menservants and maidservants, and camels." *(Genesis 12:16, NIV)* But when diseases hit the palace and Pharaoh knew where the responsibility lay, he summoned Abram and questioned him sharply and saying, " 'Take her and go!' Then Pharaoh gave orders about Abram to his men, and they sent him on his way, with his wife and everything he had."

                    Genesis 12:19-20, NIV

    Sarai was also impatient and imperious. She was barren, and once she and Abram were back in Canaan, she tried to push God's timetable, giving Abram her handmaiden, Hagar, so he might father a son. Later, when God told her it was her turn – pregnancy in old age – she laughed. And on top of it, she lied about the laughing. Even later, when she ordered Abraham to banish Hagar and Ishmael, "the matter distressed

Abraham greatly..." *(Genesis 21:11, NIV)* Ishmael was his first son, older half-brother to her late-in-life son, Isaac.

These stories and more of Sarah's (and Abraham's) family are recorded in the Book of Genesis, chapters 11-25.

You've met my mother as a singer/musician. You've met her as a maker of fine clothes, and comments about her as a teacher are peppered through the pages of this book. Those were her public faces. She wore a different face at home.

At home, everything had to be almost perfect, and just about everything needed to go Matriarch Mama's way. If Becky and I didn't wash the dishes or load the dishwasher as directed, we were mistaken. If we said we didn't like something she'd cooked, we were disrespectful. If we didn't have our beds made and our room straightened up before venturing to the table for breakfast, we were sent back to do the job over and get it right.

Mom always said her feelings were an open book. "You'll always know how I stand." Because of that, I kept the pages of my "feelings book" mostly shut. If I said what I felt, I risked her wrath. If I disagreed with her, she called me opinionated. If I made a suggestion she didn't like, I was impertinent. The cutting adjectives hurt – insolent, sassy, ungrateful.

The biggest issue between us was my weight. Mom fed me well from the beginning, but the results upset her. At five, I was chunky; at nine, solid, no waistline at all. At 18, I weighed 118 pounds and stood 5'3" tall. Better, but still not good enough. Mom weighed 98 pounds when she was married, a statistic she repeated many times.

One evening when Bob and I were dating and the house was full of company, Mom cut portions of dessert for everyone but me. When Bob noticed and asked her about my serving, she glowered and slid a smaller piece on a plate. After he left, Mom was "on my case" because my boyfriend had been sassy. Secretly, I loved the fact that he had stuck up for me. (I always wondered how she thought I could control what came out of his mouth.)

When I lived in the sorority my second year at Michigan State, Mom came by to pay a call. I was new in the house and thought that when my pager went off it meant someone had phoned. I didn't realize a visitor was waiting. One of my "sisters" ushered my mother back to the room I shared with three others. I was by myself then, though, with a cigarette smoldering on my desk. Mom didn't "smoke" immediately, but when she cornered me later, she fumed, "If I ever catch you smoking again, I'll cut off every penny for your college." I believed her. My foray with cigarettes? Just that one year on Charles St. in East Lansing.

My parents lived less than three miles from Alpha Gamma Delta, so it was possible for my mother to run into me unexpectedly. One day she drove by and spotted me walking along, enjoying spring breezes and a double-dip ice cream cone. The scowl on her face could have frozen (or melted) more than my cool treat. You'd have thought no sin was greater.

Matriarch Mama didn't like to wait for anything. When heat in the car irritated her, she immediately jacked the air conditioner to high. When my birthday neared, she almost always insisted I open my gifts two days before – on Becky's birthday – or at least on the day in between. One year she made us a cake decorated half for Becky and half for me. It was beautiful, but it wasn't all mine or all Becky's. I always felt each of us was cheated.

Guilt was another issue. My mother never shied from laying it on, even though she would have denied it if I had pointed it out. "Why wouldn't you want these clothes? I'm giving them to you." (They were clothes of hers she insisted I try on and model. I never wanted them and I certainly didn't need them, but I didn't tell her. She would never have understood and would have considered me extremely ungrateful for refusing.)

Later on, the guilt-inducing topic concerned senior living: "You kids better never put me in a nursing home. If you do, I'll haunt you. Doris and I took care of *my* mother for the last six years of her life." (Becky and I commiserated on that one in phone calls and prayed we'd never have to go that route and make such a tough decision.)

When I was in seminary in the mid-1990s, my mother insisted on twice-a-week phone calls, every Thursday and every Sunday night. It didn't matter if we had just talked. It didn't matter that there might not be anything new to discuss. It didn't matter if I had studying to do. If the calendar said Thursday or Sunday, it was time to talk. Virginia's desire. Virginia's demand.

Years later, after all of this, I realized I had been a child and an adult-child of abuse – emotional abuse by a maternal ruler. My high school friends saw the growing-up abuse much sooner than I did. Later, one of them told me, "We felt sorry for you because your mother was always trying to control you."

It never occurred to me that a person could or would act one way in public and another way at home. I never understood how my mother could bring home rave reviews from teaching and then turn around and criticize and belittle. I never knew that my mother had an obsession when it came to me.

Do we ever *fully* recover? Does the agony ever end? Only by God's grace. So much potential for good, yet so much potential for pain reside in the most primary and basic relationship – mothers and daughters, fathers and sons!

Maybe I was too thin-skinned. Perhaps a different kind of child would not have taken maternal comments or actions so seriously. Or a different kind of child would not have felt so brutalized. The results? Super-sensitivity and vigilance. My antennas were always up. When was the next thing going to happen? When would Mom put me down again?

My conclusions? My lessons learned? Parenting is the most important job in the world. Nothing else matters as much. Children are precious gifts from God. They absorb everything. They should come with instructions: Fragile. Handle With Care. Be Patient. Be Kind. Discipline, but with love. Never, ever, abuse them or neglect them.

And now, what kind of a mother have I been, you may ask. My daughter would be the person to give you an assessment.

But I do believe I have been more open to criticism than my mother was. Because of our honesty and willingness to dialogue, Marcia and I have a better relationship. I don't think I'm a maternal ruler. I take it, up to a point, when she "gets on my case." I do have a line which I won't let her cross, but until she reaches that point, I'll listen.

When I was pregnant, I vowed that if

my child was female, I wouldn't repeat the mistakes with her my mother made with me. What did I do instead? Make all kinds of mistakes of my own. In spite of them, however, Marcia and I do well together. We have been roommates, sharing crowded quarters on a family history trip to Sweden and a Caribbean cruise. I cheered for her when she ran a marathon at Disney in Orlando. I grieved with her though the death of two beloved companion cats.

Marcia teaches me things. Scrapbooking, for example. She is artistic and a detail-oriented automotive engineer. She has played the flute for thirty years. She possesses wisdom; I appreciate her advice. I give her advice, in turn, when she seeks it.

I love my daughter with all my heart. My daughter is terrific!

Thank you, God of family ties, for mothers to learn from and children to teach and learn from as well.

QUESTIONS FOR LIFE:

1. What does "matriarch" mean to you?

2. How is or was your relationship with your mother? Is she, or was she, a matriarch like Sarah? How else would you describe her?

3. How do you mother your children? What kind of example do you set?

4. How do you want your children to remember you?

5. Does your church have a matriarch? What is her personality? How would you describe her?

Be gracious in your speech.
The goal is to bring out the best in others
in a conversation,
not put them down, not cut them out.
Colossians 4:6, The Message

Michal
The Scornful One

Picture it! King David of Israel leads the ark of God into Jerusalem. He celebrates with exuberance, "wearing a linen ephod, [dancing] before the Lord ..." He and "the whole house of Israel were celebrating with all their might before the Lord..."   *2 Samuel 6:5, NIV*

Picture Michal standing at a window watching her husband "leaping and dancing before the Lord." Picture her "[despising] him in her heart."   *2 Samuel 6:16b, NIV*

When he returns home, hear her say, "How the king of Israel has distinguished himself today, disrobing in the sight of the slave girls of his servants as any vulgar fellow would!"   *2 Samuel 6:20, NIV*

Picture Michal's scorn. Her disgust.

King David responds, "It was before the Lord ... I will celebrate before the Lord. I will become even more undignified than this, and I will be humiliated in my own eyes. But by these slave girls you spoke of, I will be held in honor."   *2 Samuel 6:21-22, NIV*

"And Michal daughter of Saul had no children to the day of her death."

2 Samuel 6:23, NIV

Michal is first mentioned in 1 Samuel 14:49. Her story continues in 1 Samuel 18, 19 and 25 and 2 Samuel 3 and 6.

"You're not going to wear *that*, are you?"

I enter the living-room dressed for my date that night. My shift is lemon yellow. I think I look nice. I'm nineteen years old.

My mother's words stun me and stick in my throat, the lump refusing to budge,

59

only slowly ebbing away. I will not let her
see me cry!

Her eyes travel – slowly – from my
feet to my head.

In silence I hold my ground. I refuse
to change.

I do not remember that date.

Same living-room, twelve years later.
Now I have a daughter. We are visiting
Grandma and Grandpa.

"Your slacks are too long. You need
to shorten them," my mother says.

And about my three-year-old: "She
needs a haircut."

Come on! Don't criticize my Marcia!

My response? "Well, I guess there's
so much wrong with us we better go home."

My father eases the tension and
persuades me to stay.

I don't remember anything else about
that weekend.

Different living room. I'm a new bride, expecting my first visit from my parents. *Mom and Dad are coming! We've got to get this house straightened up!*

Bob and I are renters. We spend hours cleaning, especially sweeping cat hair from the baseboards because our landlady, now in Florida, owns a fluffy orange and white pet. But no matter how many swipes we take, evidence from that animal seeps forth. We persevere, dust, scrub and scour. We're tired, but we're satisfied.

My mother enters and looks around. She knew our house was old. She seems to approve, but then she says, "Well, your place looks nice, but you forgot to dust under your telephone table."

Sure enough, filtering morning sunshine reveals white-coated surfaces and tiny specks suspended in the air. I missed a place, and my mother finds it.

I remember nothing else about that weekend.

Every day when I was growing up, my mother "inspected" me. Her "eye travel" started when I was young. (You'd think I would have grown used to it, but I never did.) Fearing unannounced entry at dressing time, I bodily barricaded my bedroom door. (Not that my *father* would have entered without knocking.) And always, without fail, I locked the bathroom door.

With my father, Mom opened his mail. With my sister, Mom read her diary. When I commented about the postal deliveries, she said, "What's his is mine. We have a 50-50 marriage." It was her reality.

At my first wedding, I wore the gown my mother insisted we purchase. It was less

 expensive than my choice. I wore the veil she liked, secured by a bow, not the tiara-held veil I wanted and had first modeled in the store. I didn't wear my glasses, on her order, when I walked down

the aisle. "You look better without them," she said. I could have protested, but the price would have been too high. *Keep the peace, Margie, on your wedding day!*

I know my father understood my suffering. More than once he tried to get my mother to leave me alone. She never could. She never did. I was never good enough for her. My brain was good enough, but never me completely.

Ten days before Mom's death. I walk into her bedroom.

"Well, you do look better. You had gotten so hippy." (I'd lost 20 pounds since the last time I'd been in her home.)

Why did her comment sear my soul? Why did the familiar lump tighten my throat again? Why, after 59 years, should I have expected anything different, anything but another knife in my heart, another shock to my system, another high price to pay as a daughter of scorn?

And the price Mom paid, although she did not know it? The night before she died when I saw her comatose and silenced:

Now you cannot hurt me with your tongue any more!

Merciful God, please help us understand the power of our words – how much they can help and how much they can hurt.

QUESTIONS FOR LIFE:

1. How do you react to Michal's story in 2 Samuel? Why do you think she acted as she did?

2. Have you ever been the recipient of scorn? How did you feel? How did you react?

3. What do you think causes people to be scornful? Have you ever, yourself, been scornful? What were the circumstances? How do you feel about it now? (Regretfully, I have been scornful too. Some of my relatives could tell their stories.)

4. Do we repeat what we've been exposed to? How can we stop the repetition and move beyond the circumstances of our past?

"Now listen to me. I will give you counsel,
and God be with you!"

Exodus 18:19a, NRSV

Abigail
The Counselor

Have you ever helped anyone out of a jam? Abigail did. A hothead at that moment, bent on revenge, David would have committed murder if she hadn't stopped him.

David had sent emissaries to Abigail's husband, Nabal, seeking provisions for his men. David's men had been protecting Nabal's workforce, and David requested hospitality. Known even to his own servants as a wicked man, Nabal refused. One of the servants informed Abigail, realizing that when David's men reported Nabal's insult, David would take up the sword against him.

The servant said to Abigail, "Now think it over and see what you can do, because disaster is hanging over our master and his whole household." *1 Samuel 25:17, NIV*

Abigail quickly gathered two hundred loaves of bread and donkey-loads of other foodstuffs and set out to meet David. She didn't tell Nabal what she was doing.

She fell at David's feet when they met, and begged for a hearing, shouldering the blame and asking David to pay no attention to Nabal. She asked David to forgive Nabal's offense and assured him that when the Lord appointed him leader over Israel, because he had spared Nabal's life, he would "not have on his conscience the staggering burden of needless bloodshed or of having avenged himself."

Before departing from David, she said, "And when the Lord has brought my master success, remember your servant."

1 Samuel 25:31, NIV

He did. She became one of his wives after Nabal died.

This story and more about Abigail are

found in 1 Samuel 25 – 2 Samuel 2 in the Old Testament.

Her first name was Beulah, but I called her Dr. Hedahl. I started seeing her my junior year in college. By that time I was questioning my relationship with my mother, and I needed help sorting it out.

I also needed someone to talk to about my boyfriend. Bob was an interesting guy, a lover of classical music and a birding enthusiast. Our dates were unusual, like getting mired in sandy soil after a birding expedition and walking a mile to find a phone to call for a ride. (No cell phones in 1963.) Bob was interesting, but I had questions about our relationship too.

My mother's reaction to my counseling? "Well, I certainly hope you're not talking about our family!" I told her Bob was the only topic.

1974. By now I was reading books about mother-daughter relationships. *The Mother Knot* and *Like Mother, Like Daughter* are two I remember. My counselor recommended shutting off the old tapes that kept running through my mind. At first I didn't understand what she meant. Only slowly did I realize I had been pushing the play button time after time after time.

The summer following those sessions I wrote my mother a letter, seeking independence. I told her I felt like I was fighting to own my own soul. I was 31 years old. I pointed out that I was an adult woman and I deserved to be treated like one. I told her I knew she'd never cruelly criticize one of her overweight friends. She'd never belittle or scorn her.

I did not sign that letter "Love, Marg" the way I usually did. Instead, I wrote, "With hopes for a better tomorrow."

My mother told me she shook when she read the letter, and she ordered my father to read it. I never learned his reaction directly. But somehow I knew, I just knew, he understood why I said what I did. After all, he was the one who had told her, "Leave Marg alone!"

1976. After ten years of marriage Bob and I began counseling. The "group stuff" I remember I didn't care for, but the one-on-one sessions were helpful.

"You two are driving two teams of horses and you're splitting your cart apart," our one-on-one counselor told us. He predicted divorce. And even though that might have been negative for a counselor to say, I appreciated his honest assessment.

Bob and I were separated in February, 1978. Our divorce was final in May, 1979.

1981. A few months after Dad died and my anxiety had not eased, I knew I needed *something*. Tenormin had tamed my rapid heartbeat, but irregular sleep continued.

Relaxation tapes proved helpful, but not enough.

A heart attack had taken Dad in his sleep, miles from home. I received the news in a Monday morning phone call from my mother. "Your father has died." *Oh Dad, I just talked with you, and you were fine Saturday night!* As Mom's words sank in, I shook, doubled over, gut-punched by the horror story. Dad would be cremated and the cremains shipped home, but not in time for an urn to be set up at the memorial service. There would be no body, no last loving glance, no chance to say goodbye.

I thought I had to be strong for my mother so I did not cry. I stifled a scream that welled up from my toes by grabbing my hairbrush and viciously raking my scalp, stroke after stroke. I didn't care how much it hurt. I just knew I could not scream with small children in the house. Within days the tachycardia (rapid heartbeat) set in, followed by migraine headaches. My body rebelled at the grief I repressed. I sought help through counseling.

My counselor listened, but didn't say much. He soon seemed robotic. And I soon realized I was wasting more than money. Time, not counseling, was the prescription that healed my grief.

1983. Three months after Albert died, I joined a divorce support group led by a woman named Sarah. Al and I never married, but were "Camelot" companions, dating for nearly 1,000 days, a number reminiscent of John Kennedy's presidency. Al didn't qualify me for the group, but the divorce from Bob did, even though it took place in 1979. Then, too, I had lost Dad to death in 1981. In a period of less than four years I had said goodbye to the three men closest to me. Later, my daughter referred to those days as the time Mom hated "the male of the species."

I have to admit that 80 percent of men were low on my list in those days. They (some of them, anyway) cheated, they hid their feelings, and they left you. I needed other women and I needed Sarah.

A group of eight of us met under her "counselorship" in the spring that year. The others' divorces were more recent than mine so I was an anomaly. But they accepted me and we formed friendships. We liked each other so much, and felt we gained so much from Sarah, we asked for a second round of counseling. She graciously consented and even organized an autumn retreat at a farm that belonged to a friend of hers, where, besides the talking therapy, we took walks, visited the barn, were offered goat milk, and witnessed a resident tabby picking at turkey scraps on the dining-room table.

Into 1984 and beyond, we met at each others' homes, shared potluck meals, talked, laughed, joked, and continued to support one another. Our last time together was New Year's 1990, our association having lasted nearly seven years.

I lost contact with most of the group over the next two decades. But one friendship from those "Sarah days" endures. Her name is Sharon and she has blessed my life for thirty years.

1989. My mother's drinking had escalated. Anger walked with me every day. Embarrassment wrapped my shoulders. *Stop this insanity! No more saves from stumbles and bumps while leaving restaurant tables! No more slurred speech telephone conversations! No more listening to reports from Millie* (the neighbor who'd found her passed out on the living room floor). *No more answering Dr. Jones' questions about alcohol consumption.* (He questioned me the week Mom spent in the hospital dehydrated and malnourished.) *Confront her yourself about her drinking, Dr. Jones! Don't make me the go-between, clean-up person any more!* I looked to counseling yet again for answers and support.

I chose the Human Potential Center, not far from home. I liked the name, seeing it as a place of hope for people battling darkness. My counselor calmed me down, recommended Al Anon and Adult Children of Alcoholics. She also offered job advice and said that if I were going to make a move, I should do so no later than age 50.

I resigned from the newspaper ten days before my 51st birthday.

During my parish ministry years, I, too, served as a "counselor." Not in the professional sense like the counselors I've seen, but in caring conversations.

One day an elderly parishioner revealed he'd never experienced religious conversion and sought to know if that lack in his life put his standing with his Lord in jeopardy. He said he'd never known in a moment of revelation that he was a child of God. I assured him that as his pastor I had no doubts about him, and I reassured him that faith doesn't have to begin with a dramatic encounter.

The parishioner died not long after our

conversation. His family sensed he'd needed to talk with his pastor for assurance that it was "well with [his] soul."

Earlier, in the first church I served, a woman I didn't know showed up at the office one morning and asked to talk. She told me she felt weighed down by guilt, naming a denomination where she had not learned about forgiveness.

She had "sinned" in childhood and lugged the heavy guilt load ever since. Her tears told me she was repentant. Together we wept in front of the altar. I assured her she was forgiven and could lay her burden down. And then, I added gently, "No matter what you've been told in the past, God always forgives us when we repent."

I think of that woman every once in awhile and hope that she is well.

All-knowing God, please help us follow Abigail's example of graciousness, counsel and wisdom.

QUESTIONS FOR LIFE:

1. What do you think of Abigail and how she dealt with Nabal and David? Try to imagine her life – how she saw Nabal, how she saw David.

2. Have you ever seen a professional counselor? What was the catalyst that got you there? Did you receive help with your concerns and go on to a better life? How? What steps did you take?

3. Describe a time when you have been a counselor.

4. Read Psalm 1:1-3. Can we glean any principles from these verses about choosing a good counselor?

5. Why do you think some people refuse to seek help with their problems? What stops them?

There is a time for everything...
a time to be silent and a time to speak...
Ecclesiastes 3:1a, 7b, NIV

Mary, Mother of Jesus
Holding Things in Her Heart

Two sentences in the Book of Luke. Two sentences phrased almost identically, one from the time of Jesus' birth and the other from the time he was twelve years old: "But Mary treasured up all these things and pondered them in her heart." *(Luke 2:19, NIV)* "But his mother treasured all these things in her heart." (*Luke 2:51b, NIV*) Or, in the words of Eugene Peterson's *The Message*, "His mother held these things dearly, deep within herself."

What was Mary holding onto? What was she keeping safe? First, it was the news the shepherds conveyed about her newborn son, the message they had heard from the angel of the Lord that her baby was the Savior, the Christ. Second, it was information from Jesus that astonished her the day she and Joseph found him missing from their caravan and returned to Jerusalem to find him. "Didn't you know that I had to be in my Father's house?" No, Mary did not know. She did not understand. She did not know his mind – this son who had amazed the teachers in the temple courts with his knowledge and his answers.

It is possible, too, that Mary was holding onto the words old Simeon had spoken when Jesus was eight days old, the time of circumcision. Turning to her in the temple courts, he said, "This child is destined to cause the falling and rising of many in Israel, and to be a sign that will be spoken against, so that the thoughts of many hearts will be revealed. And a sword will pierce your own soul too."   *Luke 2:34-35, NIV*

How many times might she have thought, *"Who is this son that I have given birth to? What's going to happen to cause me*

so much pain? What does the future hold?"
Mary did not know, but she wondered, keeping all these things and pondering them in her heart.

Are there certain things you've never shared with anyone? Are there some things you've kept private, just to yourself? I don't mean secrets or gossip or harmful family silences, but things that might be hurtful if they were known, items better left unsaid. I also don't mean information you can't let go and stew about to the point of obsession or illness, but certain issues rightfully meant for your heart and mind alone.

One time my mother told me two things about my father I had not known when I was growing up. He had been gone for some time before she mentioned them. One item was fascinating, the other disturbing. The interesting news had to do with science, the disturbing one with behavior. The interesting piece I'm rather glad she told me, but I could have lived without knowing it. The behavior item I wish I'd never heard. It diminished my father in my eyes, even though I felt I understood it. I wish my mother had kept her own counsel and pondered that item in her heart.

I think my mother revealed those two bits of information because she was getting older and had kept them to herself for a long time. I sensed her need to unburden herself to her daughter. She gained relief, I'm sure, in the telling, but in doing so, she burdened my soul, adding an ache I would rather have lived without. To this day, it saddens me when I recall the behavioral item.

Within my own heart there are items I keep, items I hold closely. Sometimes I think about revealing them, but ultimately I choose not to because they could be hurtful. So I pray for the wisdom to keep silent and the strength to keep my knowledge to myself. Each of us is a separate individual, entitled to private thoughts and space. None of us can fully know (and perhaps should not know about) another human being. There are simply certain things rightfully known but to God.

Again, these are not secrets. Mary was not keeping secrets. She was keeping important knowledge private. Pondering, protecting a thing deeply in the heart, is not cruel or misguided or a sign of judgment gone awry. On the contrary, keeping certain things in the heart is a sign of womanly wisdom.

The Beatles affirmed it years ago in their song, *"Let It Be."*

Strengthening God, the prophet Habakkuk says you are in your holy temple. Help us be silent before you.

QUESTIONS FOR LIFE:

1. What about you? Are you a keeper or a teller?

2. Do you think this pondering aspect of Mary's life is important to duplicate as well as you can? Why or why not?

3. In your heart of hearts, what do you guard and cherish?

But from everlasting to everlasting
  the Lord's love is with those who fear him,
and his righteousness with their children's children.
                                                    Psalm 103:17, NIV

Lois
The Grandmother

A woman of sincere faith. That is how the apostle Paul portrays Lois, grandmother of his friend Timothy, his traveling companion and strong leader in the Christian church. Lois and her daughter, Eunice, Timothy's mother, were early converts to the faith, possibly through Paul's ministry in their home city of Lystra. They were women of strength, who gave Timothy a solid foundation for his work as a missionary evangelist. *2 Timothy 1:5* and *Acts 16:1* are the verses that tell their story.

My "mor mor" (Swedish for my mother's mother) was born in the province of Varmland in 1883, the seventh or eighth  child in a family of nine children. I say seventh or eighth because I don't know if Grandma or her twin, Lydia, entered the world first. Lydia died when the little girls were two.

The family lived in a downstairs corner of a large multi-family house, near a mill and a lake perfect for swimming. Great-grandpa Olaf worked in the woods, and Great-grandma Anna managed all those children.

My grandmother, Olivia, came to the United States in 1901, along with her sister, Hannah, and brothers, Karl and Anders. An older sister, Christina, had arrived earlier, and Grandma lived with Christina and helped care for her children before she and Grandpa met. A woodsman, and in time a lumber camp boss, Grandpa harvested pine in the forests of Michigan's Upper Peninsula.

Grandma and Grandpa married in 1905 and started housekeeping on the banks of the Whitefish River. In a period of fourteen years, they gave birth to seven children. The four boys arrived first. Margaret came along in 1912 and died in 1918 in the national influenza epidemic. My mother, Virginia, next to the youngest, was born in 1914. Dorothy followed in 1920.

Some time in the "nineteen teens" the family moved to Gladstone, where they settled for good. I don't know how they managed with nine people in a big house with only one bathroom, but they did.

One day, a family story goes, the boys, or some of them at least, gave Grandma a hard time. She lined them up and went down the row, boxing their ears. When she came to Clarence, the youngest, he protested, "What did I do?" She answered, "Don't worry. You'll be next."

When six-year-old Margaret died, Grandma wailed her grief. My mother was only four at the time. I've wondered for years whether Grandma's behavior frightened her or whether she suffered neglect. Dorothy replaced Margaret in Grandma's eyes, I learned later in conversations with cousins.

When I was growing up, Christmases in Gladstone were magical. Grandma cooked all day Christmas Eve to feed a crowd of more than twenty. Adults were seated at the big oval table in the dining room, older grandkids at a card table in the music room, and the youngest of us at the big rectangular table in the kitchen.

The menu was traditional Swedish and 100 percent homemade – potato sausage, head cheese, rye bread, coffee bread, lingonberries, drika (root beer), salads, boiled parsley potatoes, pickled herring, cookies for dessert, and lutefisk.

Have you ever tasted lutefisk? Have you ever heard of it? True Swedes love it. *It's a delicacy, don'tcha know?* But to me, a half-Swede, no way! Not even with the buttery white sauce that's poured over it do I consider it edible. It is lye-cured cod fish that is boiled, drained and served steaming in a large white mass, as jiggly as Santa's bowl full of jelly. And the aroma – oh my! A little like cooked cauliflower, only worse. Not on my finest day! But everything else that Grandma served was delicious.

After dinner came the gifts. And after gifts came church, 11 p.m. to midnight. All of us bundled up and settled down from the warmth and revelry to observe the "reason for the season." Great-aunts and -uncles, second cousins and friends met in the sanctuary and joined in the carols. The choir always sang *"Lyssna."* "Listen, listen, hear the angels singing..." Every Christmas I still remember *"Lyssna,"* and sing it in my heart.

On any typical day, Grandma would be up by 6 a.m. and have coffee bread, rye bread and rolls rising and two pies baked before any of us grandkids would open our eyes. The milkman would have come, driving his horse-drawn cart, carrying narrow-necked glass bottles with cream on top to the milk box on Grandma's back porch. The coffee bread with its lightly sugared crust lay sliced on a plate, soon to become the best toast in the world. And Grandpa sat at his place, waiting for granddaughter Nancy to climb in his lap and join him in eating filibunk, the sour Swedish yogurt Grandma made and kept stored in towel-covered bowls in a tin box in her pantry. Nancy wanted it with sugar; I don't know if Grandpa did.

I was four years old in 1947 when Grandma was diagnosed with cancer. It was lympho-sarcoma, which produced a lump in  her neck. Because she drank coffee by creaming it and pouring it into a saucer and sipping it over a sugar lump, I thought the cancer lump was a sugar lump that had gone down the wrong way and stuck. The doctors treated her with radium in Chicago over a period of five years, effecting a cure, and, along with our family, calling her case a miracle.

Years later, Grandma suffered painful arthritis, especially in her hands. But she didn't complain. She sat and rubbed her hands and read her Bible. She loved to read the Bible.

Grandma's family was her life. Her church was her life, too. She died at 88 and lay in her casket on her 89th birthday.

My Indiana grandmother (my father's mother) was a tall, buxom woman, one of 13 children. She was born in 1891. Her heritage was English, Scotch, and Irish, some of her ancestors having settled in Kentucky when the family first moved west. Earlier ancestors, on the East Coast, had fought in the American  Revolution. Grandma and her sister, Hazel, were proud members of the DAR (Daughters of the American Revolution).

Their maiden name was Simpson. Ulysses S. Grant, the Civil War general and 18th President of the United States, was thought to be some sort of relative, a great-uncle or a cousin. His mother's maiden name was Simpson too.

Before Grandma was married and my father was born, she taught school, all eight grades in a one-room country building. She'd attended teachers' college in Terre Haute for six weeks. One of her students was named Doyne. Because she admired him and liked his name, she named my dad, her only child, William Doyne. He went by "Willie" as a graduate student at Princeton University, but he answered to "Doyne" most of his life.

Grandma and Grandpa lived in Bainbridge, a tiny village west of Indianapolis. Their house featured a wrap-around porch, a flower garden, a big vegetable garden and a chicken coop. One day when I was five or six, Grandma killed a chicken for our dinner. She grabbed it by the neck, wrung it around hard a couple of times, axed its head off, put it down and let it run around. When it quit moving, she dunked it in scalding water and plucked its feathers. Today I consider the ritual brutal. Back then, it was the way my grandma did it.

And could she fry up a chicken! Grandma Collings was as good a cook in her way as Grandma Goodman was. Her specialties, besides chicken, were bean soup and cornbread, and best of all, cherry cobbler. My mother, a wonderful cook, couldn't bake cobbler like Grandma, and I think she was jealous when my father raved about his mother's.

Grandma never wasted anything. She taught me frugality in the kitchen. To this day, I can't throw out a leftover right away. Because of her teaching (I tell myself), I've found plastic containers with moldy contents, sometimes undecipherable, pushed to the back of a refrigerator shelf and forgotten.

I never saw Grandma Goodman wear anything but dresses. Since Grandma Collings loved to fish, her wardrobe featured variety. She stepped out of her dress and into bib coveralls, and, with pole and bucket and floppy straw hat, she set off for her favorite "hole."

She certainly didn't wear bib coveralls, though, when she campaigned in Democratic party politics. I don't know what county office she tried for, but I do know she and Grandpa staunchly supported President Franklin Roosevelt.

During the Great Depression, Grandma ran a general store. One day two barefoot children came in with a nickel. They wanted a loaf of bread. A loaf cost a dime. They walked home with the half-loaf Grandma tore and handed them.

When I was growing up, we spent far fewer Christmases in Bainbridge than we did in Gladstone. The contrast was marked. It was just the six of us – Grandma, Grandpa, Dad, Mom, Becky and me. It seemed to me the living room was too big. We didn't go to church. But we did gather around the massive black table in the dining room and dip salt from tiny cut glass bowls, drink from cut glass glasses, and serve ourselves from sparkly cut glass dishes as Grandma passed them around. I still have pieces from her collection.

Near Grandma's place at the table, a boxy brown telephone hung on the wall. It didn't have a dial. The black mouthpiece flared out in the front. The "receiver," a black flared earpiece, hung at the left side, attached not by a curly cord but by a cloth-covered  wire. When Grandma wanted to make a call, she'd crank the handle on the right side, lean close to the mouthpiece and wait for the switchboard operator to say, "Central. Number, please." It was a party line; every family had its own ring.

(Does that bring back memories? And what about today's kids? Have they ever seen that kind of telephone, even in a museum?)

By the time I was in high school, my Indiana grandparents wintered in Florida. The Christmas I was a freshman, we lived in Texas, and we traveled to Sebring for the holiday. After traditional Christmas morning gift-giving, we drove to a nearby state park for a picnic and a jitney ride, hoping to glimpse alligators lazing in the sun or mostly submerged with just their heads and beady eyes protruding from the water. Somehow Bermuda shorts and sandals didn't feel like Christmas Day.

Grandma died when she was 81. She'd had a chronic cough. She'd been lying down when Grandpa left to get the mail. He found her in a chair when he returned. It had been a fatal heart attack. They'd been married 60 years. He died a year-and-a-half later.

Officially, I am a step-grandmother, but I've been called "Grandma" all along. Patrick and Thomas are Henry's daughter's sons.

Henry and I married when Patrick was 13 months old. Since I never had a son, I found it fun to shop for little boy clothes and toys. I was entering new territory. I still am.

At 15 and 5 now, the boys are quite a contrast. Patrick's latest deal is driving. He went after his permit as soon as he could and doesn't object too much to hauling his mom and brother around in his Dodge Ram pickup. He maintains his paper route, plays the drums, and helps with the sound system at his church. He and I are rivals. He cheers for The University of Michigan always, and I for my Spartans of Michigan State.

Patrick has dark brown eyes and hair – shaved close, almost to baldness. (Not too long ago he wore it in a Mohawk. Grandpa and I wonder what style might be next.) Thomas is a butch-cut towhead. (His styles don't change as often as Patrick's.) He's in kindergarten and loves it. He's quite a sports guy too, a good dribbler with a basketball and a strong arm with a softball. At the age of two he knew a soccer ball from a basketball from a football. He also could wrestle. He'd hurl his thin but muscly little body onto Patrick and roll around on the floor without a fear in the world. Today, as the school kid, he "yucks it up" that his locker is full-size while Patrick's at the high school isn't. Now, too, he thrusts and kicks as a young student of karate.

One of my favorite memories of Patrick is taking him to his first parade. He was two years old and dressed in Oshkosh bibbed shorts. Pockets stuffed with candy the parade participants threw out, he looked like a little squirrel.

With Thomas, my favorite memory is how he doubled my name for most of a year. From age two-and-half to three-and-a-half, he called me "Gramma Gramma." I knew he'd outgrow my double name, so I cherished it as long as it lasted.

Thank you, God of the generations, for grandmothers to remember and grandchildren to love and help care for.

QUESTIONS FOR LIFE:

1. What does the relationship "grand-mother" mean to you?

2. If your grandmother(s) was part of your life long enough for you to remember, how did she treat you? What did she teach you? What do you recall about your times together?

3. Did either of your grandmothers play a role in your development of faith? How? What did they say and do?

4. If you are a grandmother yourself, what do you want your grandchildren to remember about you?

5. Why do you think the grandparent-grandchild bond most often is a good one?

When Jesus spoke again to the people, he said,
"I am the light of the world.
Whoever follows me will never walk in darkness,
but will have the light of life."

John 8:12, NIV

Mary Magdalene and Others
Followers of Jesus

Have you ever been part of a support group? Jesus had one, and I don't mean the disciples. Jesus' support group consisted of women. Some of them provided for him out of their own means (maybe brought home the "bacon" and paid the bills). Others followed him to his death, to the foot of the cross and the garden tomb. *Matthew 28:1-10, Mark 15:40-41, 15:47, 16:1-11, Luke 8:2-3, 23:49, 23:55-56, 24:1-11, John 19:25, 20:1-18*

Some of their names we know – Mary

Magdalene, Mary the mother of James, Joanna, Salome. Some of their names we don't know. They worked behind the scenes in Jesus' ministry. They accompanied him and served him. He blessed their lives by his touch.

I have not seen the hit musical *"Church Basement Ladies."* I would like to, but I don't *need* to because I have five church basement ladies of my own: my maternal grandmother, her sister-in-law and three sisters, four great-aunts to me. They were followers of Jesus, a support group for their families and their church.

Their names resonate with the sound of "a" – Anna, Olivia Augusta, Emma Sofia, Johanna (Hannah) Mathilda, Hilda Josefina. The final four were born in "The Old Country" and emigrated to the United States between 1900 and 1905.

●Aunt Emma, the oldest, wore her hair pulled back tightly in a bun, not a strand out of place. She sat ramrod straight (maybe it was her corset), and she rarely smiled. Visiting her house when I was small, I never knew what I might encounter. Would her expression be stern that day? Fright gripped my little soul. I didn't want to bump into her end table or accidentally chip or crack a china coffee cup. With the Swedes, you see, it was always coffee, never tea.

●Aunt Hannah was the jolly one. Unlike Emma, she smiled a lot and her home was warm and welcoming. I remember aromas of something wonderful always simmering on the stove.

On Christmas Eve, while the dishes were being done, before the time for gifts, Grandma would send my cousin Jane and me out in the dark and the snow. Our Aunt Dorothy drove us to deliver a loaf of homemade bread or some freshly baked cookies to Hannah's house. Or maybe it was a box of butter mints Aunt Dorothy had picked up from a store in Chicago. I remember climbing Aunt Hannah's front-porch steps bundled against the winter wind, and from her entryway seeing twinkling tree lights and hearing talk and laughter, most often from Aunt Hannah's husband, Carl, and her brother, Andrew.

● Aunt Hilda was Grandma's telephone sister. They talked every day, taking a break from their household chores, chattering mostly in Swedish. My cousins, my sister and I, sitting on the floor playing in the music room near Grandma's phone, eavesdropped on their conversations, not understanding anything until suddenly an English word grabbed our attention. We thought it was funny, a word we knew popping up every so often.

● Aunt Anna I didn't see very often or know very well. But she must have had a great sense of humor. One family story recounts the day she dressed herself in a granddaughter's band uniform, complete with plumed hat and strap under chin, and marched around the back yard when that granddaughter got home from school. A photo shows an impish grin on Aunt Anna's face.

She also sewed superbly, copying the latest designs in fashion magazines. She pieced together many skirts and dresses for her daughters.

From their Mission Covenant Church in Gladstone, these five proper Swedish ladies followed Jesus. They organized and supervised church basement activities, helping with anything and everything, especially funeral dinners. The menu might have varied, but one item was always present – Swedish meatballs, lovingly made from scratch. Today those dear ladies probably roll in their graves. The church women buy the meatballs from Gordon's!

Grandma and her women kinfolk attended worship regularly. One winter day after the service, they posed on the front steps of the church, looking like quintuplets, in black boots, black coat, black hat, gloves, and black purse draped over an arm – simply their garb, and the proper way to dress for church in the early 1950s.

We, in the third and fourth generations, have kept that photo. It is a  gem we cherish. Those young immigrants from Sweden left the land they knew, ventured forth to the New World, trusting the providence of God. I call them our family's church basement ladies, our "Church Steps Ladies" as well.

God of the ages and family heritage, thank you for dedicated older women for younger women to learn from.

QUESTIONS FOR LIFE:

1. What does it mean to be a follower of Jesus?

2. Who in your family follows him?

3. Do you have any great-aunts? If so, what are your favorite stories about them, your favorite memories of them? What influence have they been in your life?

4. Do you have any photos of them? What does the photo reveal and how does it match your memory or knowledge or them?

5. Would you call your great-aunts a kind of support group? Why? Who do they support, and how?

6. Do you receive support from others? Do you give support to others? Describe the situations.

"Now therefore revere the Lord,
   and serve him in sincerity and faithfulness" ...
                              Joshua 24:14a, NRSV

Jehosheba
Heroic Aunt

What a find – Jehosheba! I had not known her story. What did she do? Simply perform a rescue, save her nephew from death at the hands of his grandmother, hide him for six years and thereby save a dynasty.

Joash was a prince in Judah in the days when kings ruled the land. After his father, King Ahaziah, died of battle wounds, the king's mother, Athaliah, "proceeded to destroy the whole royal family." But Jehosheba, King Ahaziah's sister, "took Joash ... and stole him away from among the royal princes, who were about to be murdered." She hid him and his nurse "... for six years while Athaliah ruled the land."

2 Kings 11:1-3, NIV

When Joash was seven years old, "he began to reign." *(2 Kings 11:21, NIV)* His grandmother's attempt to kill all of Ahaziah's sons failed because his Aunt Jehosheba intervened. In doing so she not only saved him but helped fulfill God's promise *(2 Samuel 7)* that the Messiah would be born through King David's descendants.

Joash ruled Judah for forty years, repairing the temple and preserving the "seed" of David, the ancestry of Jesus.

Jehosheba's story is told in *2 Kings 11:1-3* and *2 Chronicles 22:9c-12*. Joash's story continues through *2 Kings 12*.

Would you call any of your aunts heroic? Were or are any of them heroines in your life?

As far as I know, none of my aunts

rescued anyone, but they all left imprints. And if nobility of character is part of the definition of heroine, my aunts, indeed, were heroic.

 • Aunt Vi I knew the least. She died in 1967. But when I was a child, I thought  she was exotic with her dark brown hair and eyes. A large purple birthmark on the right side of her face might have been off-putting to a child, but it wasn't for me. Aunt Vi always greeted me with a smile and asked me about school. She taught 4th grade for many years.

 She was the mother of my only cousin by adoption. I don't know that she and Uncle Mike "rescued" Jeff from the orphanage, but they opened their hearts, made him their son and gave him a home. I wish I had known them better.

 • Aunt Astrid stood tall, slim and blonde. (Have you heard her name before? Maybe, if your heritage is Swedish.) She bore four children in thirteen years. She served her church as choir director and pianist and started many of her private piano students with John Thompson songs and scales. (If you took piano lessons, you might remember selections from those big John Thompson red books.)

At one point she and her family lived in Grand Haven, on Michigan's west coast.  Their huge house sat on a hill, not far from the Lake Michigan beach. A brick retaining wall nearly hid the house from the street. I don't know if an intercom system (no cell phones and texting in those days) helped with communication, but without one, Aunt Astrid and Uncle Cliff might have had to "round up and shout" to corral their "chilluns" to the table.

I loved spending time with Aunt Astrid in her big, high-ceilinged kitchen. I liked to watch her cook. I don't remember what we talked about, but she never seemed to mind having me hang around. Like Aunt Vi, she asked me about school. And she let me set the table, a much bigger one than we had at home. I wanted to make sure I put everything in exactly the right position.

Was she heroic? In my young eyes, yes. Or as the Swedes sometimes say, "You betcha!"

● Aunt Ella lived on a farm. I didn't know her very well when I was growing up. My sister and I were the "city cousins" from 450 miles away.

She grew up in North Dakota and met Uncle Will when she was teaching school in a tiny town in the Upper Peninsula. Uncle Will and a buddy heard about two pretty teachers and went to take a look. Marriage and five children  followed, and after years as a homemaker and mother, Aunt Ella earned a master's degree and returned to teaching.

Her farmhouse kitchen was dysfunctional, according to her daughter, Patsy. Back and forth, back and forth across too much floor space her mother traveled, from ice box to sink to wood-burning stove with metal pipe angled up through the wall. Aunt Ella roasted and baked for her big family and steamed ear after ear of sweet corn for extended family noshing contests every summer.

Aunt Ella and I talked after my father's memorial service. He died in March, 1981, two days into spring. I must have mentioned spring because Aunt Ella said, "Calves frolic in the springtime, you know. They kick up their heels." City girl that I was, I did not know that.

Life on a farm gave Aunt Ella that knowledge, of course. It seemed to me she knew that, as the psalmists say, God's creatures express the joy of being alive, especially in the springtime. If robins wake up and greet the day with a trill near 5 a.m., why wouldn't calves kick up their heels?

> ... for now the winter is past,
> the rain is over and gone.
> The flowers appear on the earth;
> the time of singing has come,
> and the voice of the turtledove
> is heard in our land.
>
> *Song of Songs 2:11-12, NRSV*

Aunt Ella's comment about calves triggered memory of those verses from the Bible.

She died in October 1995, during my second year in seminary. She knew I was on my way to becoming a pastor. It didn't surprise her. She didn't tell me directly, but Patsy told me her mother supported me. She saw something in me I hadn't seen in myself. I am forever grateful.

● Aunt Dorothy was my mother's younger sister. She was married when I was five. I can still see her coming down the stairs in Grandma and Grandpa's house in her pale pink honeymoon dress, "fancied up" with buttons from neckline to waist. Her shoulder-length light brown hair soft-curled and framed her face. I thought she looked like a princess. She was so pretty!

Aunt Dorothy taught kindergarten. One time – I think I was three – she let me visit her class. And it was she who fixed me up one day in a short  drum majorette outfit, complete with baton and tall hat. I still have the picture and treasure it to this day.

Sadly, in later years, health problems plagued Aunt Dorothy. Peripheral neuropathy was most painful. She died in 1981 at the age of 60.

• Aunt Doris lived the longest of my five aunts. She was going on 96 when God took her home in the spring of 2006. With that longevity, my memories go deep.

One Christmas I gave her a red plastic tomato with a green top. Guess what! It held ketchup. She used it for years. It amazed me it didn't wear out, and she kept it all her life.

Aunt Doris and I shared the love of maps. We reminisced about places we'd visited, and one day we spread out a map on her living-room carpet and pored over it on our hands and knees.

I think a lot of us in the family saw Aunt Doris as the glue that held us together.

 She always helped out. She housed out-of-towners for funerals. She hosted Christmas dinner, treating and seating almost as many of us as Grandma did on Christmas Eve. She supported her church. She took everything in stride – quietly, unassumingly, without making judgments. Aunt Doris had a "sweet tooth" but never gained weight. She also liked teddy bears. I gave her one for her 80th birthday and remember thinking it was really neat that an "old woman" (80 seemed old to me then) had a bear collection.

Aunt Doris encouraged me to write. And she outlived two husbands.

These are my aunts. Can you tell that I loved them? Were they heroines? Maybe. Maybe it depends on your definition.

My mother, of course, was my cousins' aunt. They called her Aunt Ginny. They also called her Auntie Mame. To them, she was colorful, funny and dramatic.

The night Cousin Debbie was married and the family rented a block of motel rooms, Mom paraded down the hallway to Aunt Doris's room in bright red satin pajamas. I was mortified. Other family members thought it was a "stitch." Mom's comment to me, "What's the matter? I'm fully covered up." And she told Cousin Jane there would have been nothing wrong with walking down that hallway in a slip. The next Christmas, Jane and her sister, Nancy, sent Mom a thick red bathrobe to wear over those pajamas.

My cousins knew the name of Aunt Ginny's favorite restaurant. There was no better place on earth than Hershey's in East

Lansing for prime rib. Auntie Mame said it was so! The salad bar, with plates chilled to perfection, featured all kinds of goodies. In later years, when Mom had trouble walking there on her own, she asked me or a niece to fill her plate, always with hard-boiled egg and Michigan dried sweet cherries.

Auntie Mame knew her mind and delighted many of her kinfolk.

I became an aunt myself in 1974. I have two nieces and one nephew. These days, sadly, our paths do not cross. Two live in Texas, one in Florida. I haven't seen two of them since their father died in 2005. I pray, however, that in our contacts in the past Aunt Margie made a good impression.

Caretaker God, thank you for faithful aunts who leave legacies of love for their nieces and nephews.

QUESTIONS FOR LIFE:

1. Does Jehosheba's story mean anything to you? What is your reaction? Was she a hero? What made her heroic?

2. Does her story help you think about your aunts? What did they or what do they bring to your life? Do any of their stories inspire you? Which ones, and why?

3. If you are an aunt yourself, how do you want to be remembered?

4. What is your definition of "hero"? (Hebrews, Chapter 11, mentions heroes of the faith. What made these people heroic? How did their faith affect their families? How does your faith affect your family?)

How very good and pleasant it is
when kindred live together in unity!

Psalm 133:1, NRSV

Elizabeth
Cherished Cousin

Cousin or aunt? Luke does not specify Elizabeth's relationship to Mary. Instead, he calls her a "relative." *(Luke 1:36)* Does it matter? No, not overall. But yes, it matters for the purposes of this book. It also matters because I'd grown up having learned that the two women were cousins, and it's hard to give up a cherished old identity for a new one. Just recently I learned that in Islam, Elizabeth is considered to have been Mary's aunt.

What truly matters in Luke's telling of the story is that the younger Mary had an older woman to turn to, spend time with and lean on, an older woman with whom to share her stunning news. Mary "hurried" to Elizabeth's house and stayed about three months.

Can you imagine all the women had to talk about, both pregnant unexpectedly? Can you imagine what Elizabeth could tell Mary about what she might feel as her pregnancy progressed? And imagine all the help Mary could provide Elizabeth as her older cousin grew larger with child. Imagine all the joy they shared in waiting and expectation.

Luke, the doctor, is unique in narrating this story of pregnancy and kinship.

Luke 1:39-56

Jane is my Elizabeth. She is three years older than I. We share a special bond that dates from childhood.

Why she was so good to me when we were growing up, I do not know. But I never felt like a tag-along, and we could always talk.

When I was 12, I broke my arm. Jane and Linette, another cousin, had taken me horseback riding. I'd been on the trail near my grandparents' home in Gladstone only once before, and I didn't remember the hill or the need to rein in my mare at the bottom. She veered right, I fell left and landed on my left arm. Jane helped me mount her again, and led  her as we walked the mile back to the stable. Even a canter was too much. I cradled my arm against each movement and tried to stifle moans and screams, all the while praying that my shoulder was dislocated and my arm not broken.

But broken it was, and not just any break. The emergency room doctor in Escanaba had not seen a break like mine before, the humerus split clean through, two inches from the shoulder socket. He did his best to set it, but three days later X-rays showed the bones had slipped.

Back home in East Lansing, my father immediately took me to an orthopedic surgeon. My break challenged even him. At first he encased me in plaster, a body cast, the broken arm angled over my head. He wanted to keep me out of the hospital and let me heal at home. But wrapped in stiff white from my chest to my hips, I couldn't bend, I couldn't turn and I couldn't get out of bed by myself. Nurses lifted me to my feet. The cast added pounds, and walking weighed me down. I felt dizzy and off balance. I wondered how I'd be able to manage when the doctor sent me home.

He didn't. The body cast didn't work. An X-ray showed the bones had slipped again. This time, the surgeon settled on traction, attaching my arm with pulleys to sandbags dangling from a steel frame over my bed. Positioning my upper arm at a 90-degree angle to my lower arm, he inserted a pin through my elbow to secure the suspension system. I spent the month of August 1955 strung up, lying on my back in St. Lawrence Hospital in Lansing, Michigan, one of the hottest Augusts the city ever endured.

Three attempts over ten days to set a broken arm!

One especially muggy day, Jane visited me in the hospital. She was 15, vacationing with her family in Lower Michigan. Her visit cheered me up, but what I remember most is her clothes. Her poodle skirt with huge crinoline, saddle shoes, and belt cinched at the waist made the coolest outfit I'd ever seen. (What she was wearing wowed me!) I wished I could wear clothes like she did. She kept up with the latest styles, and to my younger eyes, that meant she was totally "with it."

She was "with it," too, when it came to music. *"The Bells of St. Mary's"* and Johnny Mathis's version of *"The Twelfth of Never"* were topping the charts. Mathis may not have been Elvis, but he had his share of screaming fans. Listening to those ballads, Jane and I were in their number, love-sick teen-age girls, swooning with romantic dreams.

One Labor Day weekend when we were in college, Jane tried to teach me to water ski. She'd known how for years, spending hours swimming and skiing in Gladstone's Lake Michigan bay, lifeguarding and sunning at the beach. She and her friends gave good instructions, shouting encouragement across the waves, but I stood upright on those skis only a very few seconds.

Also in our college days, Jane introduced me to Bergie – tall, handsome blue-eyed blond, a simply stunning Swede. He was a high school friend of hers, not her boyfriend, so it was okay if I went "head over heels." We didn't date during that Christmas vacation, but we did play cards and board games at parties. When I returned to Michigan State and he returned to Northern Michigan University and I spent New Year's Day alone and couldn't see him anymore, I thought I'd die. I fought back tears, swallowed the lump in my throat, and pushed the iron over broadcloth blouses so hard it's a wonder I didn't burn them. All day, New Year's Day, getting clothes ready to return to classes, I ached and sighed for the man I wanted – Jane's friend, from her hometown.

In 1971, Jane and I, like Elizabeth and Mary, shared pregnancy at the same time. I gave birth to Marcia in February. Jane birthed her son, Jon, in September. At our grandmother's funeral the next January we shared stories about our babies and learned that Grandma had been able to hold each of them before she died. We cherished the memory that she had been able to do that with each of her great-grandchildren.

July 2002 brought a family history trip to Sweden. Jane and I joined ten other American cousins, all craving to dig deeper into ancestral roots in Nykroppa in the province of Varmland. Our host group of sixteen cousins met us at a museum complex not far from town.

Some of us Americans were first cousins to each other but second cousins at the closest to the Swedes. As we compared notes and amended our genealogy charts, third and fourth and even fifth cousins got acquainted. And oh, the Swedes put us

Americans to shame. All but the youngest of them spoke fluent English.

They served us a typical luncheon featuring meatballs and boiled potatoes; carrots, fresh from a garden; pear juice with blueberries; pickled beets; hardtack; lingon-berries; cheese, and currant cake with cream. We exchanged photos and gifts, shared jokes and sang songs. Then later, with one Swedish cousin as a guide, we walked the land where the old homestead stood, stepping gingerly near the foundation and hearing the water rush over the rocks in the river nearby. We tried to imagine what our grandmothers experienced more than a century before.

We also tried to picture their leaving Sweden as we posed for a photo at the train station from which they departed. Standing on the tracks, we wondered how long their emigration journey had taken – from Nykroppa to Goteborg to New York by steamship and finally to Gladstone, Michigan, in the U.S.A.

Jane and I, both in our golden years now, phone and see each other as often as we can. We look forward to family reunions and Fourth of July celebrations in Gladstone, where she grew up and I spent some of my happiest vacations.

Thank you, dear God, for my "cherished Elizabeth" and for the rich heritage of cousins in my life.

QUESTIONS FOR LIFE:

1. Is there an Elizabeth in your life? Who is she, and what makes her special? What makes you cherish the relationship? What special memories do you have of her?

2. Do you have other cousins? How have they influenced you? What do you remember most about your times together?

3. Psalm 133:1, the lead-in verse to this chapter, mentions kinfolk living together in unity. Has unity been your experience with your relatives? Why or why not?

Let love be genuine;
hate what is evil, hold fast to what is good;
love one another with mutual affection;
outdo one another in showing honor.
Romans 12:9-10, NRSV

Ruth

Faithful Daughter-in-law

"Intreat me not to leave thee,
or to return from following after thee:
for whither thou goest, I will go;
and where thou lodgest, I will lodge:
thy people shall be my people,
and thy God my God:
Where thou diest, will I die,
and there will I be buried:
The Lord do so to me, and more also,
if ought but death part thee and me."
Ruth 1:16-17, KJV

R uth spoke these words to her mother-in-law, Naomi, who had just told Ruth and her sister-in-law, Orpah, to return to their mothers' homes and, hopefully, find new husbands someday. The three of them were widows in the land of Moab, where Naomi and her husband and two sons had gone to live years before when famine struck their town of Bethlehem in Judah. The sons had married Moabite women – Ruth and Orpah – and lived there about ten years, but death had taken all three men.

The famine, meanwhile, came to an end, and Naomi decided to go home. Ruth and Orpah said they would go with her, but she urged them not to, telling them their chances for remarriage would be much better if they stayed where they were. She persuaded Orpah, who kissed her goodbye, "but Ruth clung to her," the Bible says.

Once more, Naomi urged Ruth to go back. But Ruth had made her decision.

"Don't urge me to leave you or to turn back from you," she insisted. *Ruth 1:16, NIV* Or, in the words of the King James Bible:

"Intreat me not to leave thee..."

"So the two women went on until they came to Bethlehem." *Ruth 1:19a, NIV*

Thus the story begins in the Old Testament book that bears Ruth's name.

I never did get it right. I never did learn to make a perfect pie crust.

More than once, my mother-in-law, Marie, tried to teach me, showing me the way to stir the mixture so it would hang together without leaving flour  specks on the sides of the bowl. Showing me the way to roll the dough to an eighth of an inch and keep the cracks out. Showing me how to lift it into the pan and crimp the edges to achieve the fluted look. And she taught me how long a cherry pie should bake, as well as an apple pie and a peach. I might S-curve slit the top crust, she said, and add smaller slits at various places. Marie tried to help me make a pie crust to "melt in your mouth." I never did get the knack, flunking Pie Crust 101. I hope I didn't disappoint my mother-in-law with my lack of baking ability.

Marie was a home economist, a nutritionist, a wonderful cook. She did not cook fancy or gourmet (except for the pies), but "good for you," sensibly, tastefully. She set an attractive table. Sometimes she'd have her sons help her.

Marie was also a gardener, a canner, a preserver. Nothing was to be wasted. One hot August day when Bob and I were canning tomatoes, he told me he'd learned the skill from his mother.

Marie loved classical music. Mozart was her favorite. She loved wild flowers and birds. Bob always credited his mother for his love of birds and his specializing in ornithology.

Mother's Day weekend in the late 1960s found Bob and me, Marie and her good friend, Marian, in southern Ontario, hiking the woods and Lake Erie shoreline at Point Pelee National Park, trying to spot the black-throated blue warbler and other colorful species the three of them had heard. Little old ladies with binoculars? Marie and Marian for sure. Birding hats on heads, they toted well-thumbed bird books – in all kinds of weather. Sun or rain, soaking wet or sunburned, we never missed Point Pelee that second weekend in May for the spring migration. It was *the place* for birders (and birds) to be, a temporary shelter for species that crossed the Great Lake and rested before flying farther north. I learned to love the birds (grackles and starlings excepted) from my mother-in-law and her son.

Marie was also a traveler and a reader. She and Marian enjoyed ElderHostel, visiting Germany and Scandinavia as well as sites in the U.S.A.

The Christian Science Monitor topped her newspaper list. She liked its balanced reporting and detailed coverage of events. She clipped articles she thought would interest Bob and me, and after our divorce, she still sent items my way. Over the years, we kept our friendship. She died in April, 2008, just shy of her 91st birthday.

I often thought of Marie as my second mother. She understood me. When I wrote her a letter, often I'd write it to Marian too, because they made their home together and Marian and I were friends. I'd start the letter, "Dear M and M." With my name of Margaret and my daughter's name of Marcia, I liked to think of the four of us as "Emmy" winners.

I was blessed to have Marie in my life for 45 years. I hope I blessed her life too. No mother-in-law jokes for me. She loved me and I loved her. She called me the daughter she never had. (She had lost a baby girl – carried to term but stillborn.)

Thank you, loving God, for bonds of kinship that transcend blood and enrich the heart.

QUESTIONS FOR LIFE:

1. Are you a daughter-in-law? If so, what is (or was) your relationship with your husband's mother? What have you learned from her?

2. If your relationship with your mother-in-law isn't what you wish it to be, what might you do to make it better?

3. What would have been some challenges Ruth faced as she followed Naomi to an unfamiliar country?

4. Why do you think Ruth made the decision to stay with Naomi?

5. What are your reactions to the story of these two women?

Lydia
The Believer

The story is short, only three verses in the Book of Acts. Lydia, a business-woman in Philippi, listens to Paul's message about Jesus. She responds with an open heart, is baptized along with her household, and invites Paul and his traveling companions to her home. "If you consider me a believer in the Lord, come and stay at my house," she said. "And she persuaded us," Luke wrote.

Such a short, short story about the first person to become a Christian in Europe.

Acts 16:13-15, NIV

Sodden. So rainy the wipers struggled to keep up. But a trip to town couldn't be delayed. Supplies needed to be restocked at the camp on August 3, 1974.

Mickey was driving. She and I became friends that summer in northern Wisconsin, at the National Audubon Camp near Sarona. I found her easy to talk to, an older woman who listened and didn't make judgments. She directed the waterfront and taught canoeing, and she told the cook she'd be glad to pick up some last-minute groceries.

The last two months had been tough for me. My last grandparent had died – my handsome, white-haired Indiana grandpa, nearly 89 years old. I felt my marriage falling apart and found myself bitter about my husband's behavior. Into Mickey's listening ears I poured out the frustrations of that miserable summer, complaining about how Bob had treated me. He and Marcia and I were at the camp because he was on the staff, teaching ornithology.

I don't remember how long I carried

on, but after a while I stopped talking about Bob and started talking about myself. I know I sighed as we neared town, trying to come to terms with everything, and I said, "You know, Mickey, there's so much love inside me that's just bursting to get out." She responded slowly. "I believe you, Marg, but first you have to get rid of all that hate."

She wasn't being cruel, but I was shocked, very much taken aback. *What do you mean? I'm **not** full of hate.* Then, looking down, I saw that my hands were balled into fists. Mickey went on. "You know, Marg, God loves you. God loves you through everything and forgives you when you repent."

Errands accomplished and lunch finished, we headed back to camp. The day began to clear. Mickey parked on grass, down the hill from the dining hall, and we sat for several minutes before getting out of the car. Maybe because I'd gone to church with her a few times, she asked me if I'd like to pray. I hadn't done much of it on my own in the last ten years and certainly not with just one other person. I felt uncomfortable and realized I was inwardly squirming. But I said I'd listen if she prayed. When she finished, we sat silent. It had been an emotional day. I had spewed out so much, and Mickey had accepted it all. As we watched and mused awhile, a bluebird appeared and perched on a post at the edge of the parking area. Tears came to my eyes.

That evening after dessert, during coffee and conversation, brilliant sunshine streamed through the western windows, sending rays across our table. And I knew, I simply knew, that the messages of the day had come together and God was cracking my heart.

It's true. It's true. God loves me! Jesus does too! What Mickey said is true. Although I hadn't thought of them in years, the words to *"Jesus Loves Me"* suddenly came back.

If anyone had been looking at me at the table that evening, they might have thought I'd gone crazy. I grinned from ear to ear, and I couldn't wait to run and tell

Mickey. I also couldn't wait to tell Russ, a biology instructor at the camp. He'd attended the country church near Sarona with Mickey and me that summer, and I knew he was a dedicated Christian, a professor at Wheaton College in Illinois. In his gentle, quiet way, Russ was an example of everything a Christian should be. He was the most Christ-like person I have ever met.

When I found him in his dorm room before sunset, I asked him almost frantically to point me to the story of the woman in the Bible who was forgiven, not the woman Jesus had saved from stoning (*John 8:1-11),* but the woman who had wept at his feet, wiped them with her hair and poured perfume on them.   *Luke 7:36-50*

As soon as I entered my room, I grabbed my Bible and read the passage. Overwhelmed, I fell across my bed and cried, sobbing, not being able to believe the love lavished by my God and my Christ. Yes, *my* God and *my* Christ, unlike they had been before, no longer just in my head but in my heart.

And then more words came to my mind:

"Amazing grace, how sweet the sound
That saved a wretch like me.
I once was lost, but now am found,
Was blind, but now I see.

"T'was grace that taught my heart to fear,
And grace my fears relieved.
How precious did that grace appear
The hour I first believed."

I had grown up in the church, been baptized Presbyterian and attended Presbyterian Sunday School as a child. I'd sung in my mother's youth choir. I'd spent Sunday nights at Youth Fellowship during high school and Sunday afternoons in Rhythmic Choir (a liturgical dance group). I even preached one-third of a Youth Day sermon. I studied for a year in Affirmation Seminar before Confirmation Day. But somehow all this wonderful training had not penetrated my heart. Head, yes, for all those years, but never deep in my heart.

That August day in Wisconsin changed everything.

"Jesus loves me, this I know.
For the Bible tells me so."

"What a wonderful change
in my life has been wrought
Since Jesus came into my heart!"

Thank you, transforming God, for your power and love that turn lives around forever.

QUESTIONS FOR LIFE:

1. What do you think of Lydia's short story?

2. Do you believe in Jesus? Describe who he is to you.

3. Is Jesus in your head? Is he in your heart? What is the difference between a "head" knowledge of Jesus and a "heart" knowledge?

4. How many different words can you think of to describe Jesus of Nazareth?

Answer me when I call to you,
O my righteous God.
Give me relief from my distress;
be merciful to me and hear my prayer.
Psalm 4:1, NIV

Naomi
The Desperate One

Widowed. Both sons dead. Living in a foreign land. Could life have been much harder for Naomi? How would she and her daughter-in-law, Ruth, make it across the desert back to Bethlehem now that the famine was over? If they managed to survive, what would life be like once they were home?

Naomi said the Lord's hand had gone out against her. She said her name should be Mara, which means bitter. "I went away full, but the Lord has brought me back empty. Why call me Naomi? The Lord has afflicted me; the Almighty has brought misfortune upon me."

"So Naomi returned from Moab accompanied by Ruth, the Moabitess, her daughter-in-law, arriving in Bethlehem as the barley harvest was beginning."

Ruth 1:21-22, NIV

With those words, Chapter I ends. But what comes next? Why is the barley harvest mentioned? Chapters II, III, and IV contain the answers and much more in the Book of Ruth.

Naomi was desperate. So was I. Her situation could not have been much worse. Neither could mine. But unlike her, I did not blame the Lord for my misfortune. It was not the Almighty's hand that had gone out against me but my own.

Fall of 1985. My mother, who has left Michigan for her condo in Florida, comes down with diverticulitis. It lasts all winter. A Florida friend of hers calls me. "You have to do something about your mother!" I feel like screaming. *She's down there; I'm up here (in Michigan). What do you want me to do?* Fortunately, Mom recovers.

The Ides of March 1986. A drunk driver totals my pretty white Citation. The seatbelt bruises my belly. My "shiner" is deep purple-black. My pea-green Plymouth replacement turns out to be a lemon. Bad choice to buy a car from my ex-husband's community college colleague.

May of 1986. My body is telling me something is wrong. Maybe there's more ac-cident damage than I know.

Hysterectomy surgery takes place in June. Six weeks later, I return to work. Pain pierces my back and radiates down my right leg. All my sick leave is gone. I sit at my dining table and cry. I'm scared and angry and miserable.

The surgeon says it's a bulged disc, sends me to bed for three days, and pre-scribes nine pills to fight the swelling. The pills do their job and despite my lingering pain, I'm ready for physical therapy. When I ask both orthopedist and family doctor about pain medication, they refuse me. I feel like neither cares how much I hurt, and neither will say how long I can expect the pain to last.

August 1986. Agony accompanies work. How long can I keep going? More time off is not an option. I have myself and my daughter to support. I'm desperate, despairing. The hysterectomy was one thing, the back pain another.

The local village doctor I turn to prescribes Xanax, defined in his medical dictionary as a "mildly addictive muscle relaxer." The label says take two. I do that – at first. Then, not knowing why, I up it to three, four, then five, until I'm downing seven little white pills every day.

By the end of October, anxiety replaces back pain, and sleep is sporadic. One night it comes easily, however, and I decide to stop the Xanax. I don't tell the doctor. My heart pounds, thudding in my chest. I grow paranoid and fight panic. Withdrawal has set in and I do not know it. I do not know a person needs to be weaned off Xanax. I fear crying at any moment. I fear losing my memory too, so I frantically write everything down. I'm not hungry and do not eat.

Finally, not knowing what else to do, I talk with my pastor, whose wife has had drug issues. He suggests I get help. Despite the drug fog, I know he's right. I call a hospital in nearby Toledo. I'm told to eat and urged to get there as fast as I can. It is the first of November.

That rainy, miserable Saturday my ex-husband and daughter drove me twenty miles to the center of Toledo. Little did I know what was coming. All I wanted to do was sleep.

After admission, I was given Valium. I found that hilarious, giving me one mood-altering drug to replace another. I didn't think it would work, but I was wrong. I slept until noon on Sunday.

By Tuesday all the paperwork and insurance were in place. Late that afternoon a van transported me from the hospital to the Alcoholism Treatment Center, an old, high-ceilinged hotel in another part of town. That night I was given a room of my own near the nurses' station, and I thought, *This is nice. It's quiet. I'm safe.*

My comfort was not to last. Staff nurses transferred me the next night to a room near the game room. I had a roommate and could hear the conversations and the pool balls smacking each other way after I longed to be asleep. But sleep turned out to be a precious and scarce commodity in that ATC. The Valium had been for one night only, and the Xanax lingering in my body kept me awake night after night.

Day after day, I wondered how I could keep functioning without sleep. Frightened, I fought rising panic. But the night nurses were kind when I approached them in the wee hours, and they pointed me to the library where I could sit and read.

Daytime was busy with lectures,

relaxation exercises and recreation. Each night held a meeting, most often AA. My Xanax was considered dry booze. I prayed hard at those meetings that I wouldn't get a headache from all the smoke in the room, and in my heart I wished that Alcoholics Anonymous would help people quit cigarettes as well as drinking.

Beer drinkers, winos, crack addicts, coke snorters and heroin users resided in the center along with me. No matter what substance we had abused, we were lumped together. One day, toward the end of treatment, when some of the folks were soon to be released, one man had to face the harsh truth. He would die. He allowed the counselors to share his story in a seminar one morning. He had done so much damage with drinking that the end was near. He simply would not recover.

Another day, one of the men asked me what I was doing there. I told him I'd become addicted to a prescription medication. He just shook his head. I thought it best not to ask his story. Two thick gold chains around his neck had me guessing about his addiction. I wondered whether he might have been dealing as well as using.

Yet another day the prescription called for swimming. I've always loved to swim and was comfortable doing lazy strokes, treading water, and floating. One of the men, clinging to the side of the pool in the deep end, watched me float, arms extended, and asked me how I could do that. "I trust the water to hold me up," I said. And even in that place, recovering from addiction, I knew the Lord God was with me, holding me up and supporting me even more than the water.

One weekend they allowed us go home. The directions were strict. No medications of any type were to be taken, not even one aspirin. We would be drug tested as soon as we returned. I prayed I wouldn't get a headache over those two days or be tempted to go to a bar for a drink. I feared if I were addicted to "dry booze," I might be addicted to wet booze, too, and not be able to avoid it, even though I had not been a heavy drinker. The lecturers simply had me frightened and distrusting my own behavior.

Monday morning at announcement time after that weekend of freedom, the director called my name. She summoned me to her office and sternly asked,"Did you use anything over the weekend?" My urine test had come back suspicious. Shaking my head, simply stunned, I denied taking anything, and I was so upset I cried. Apparently residual Xanax still lingered in my body. It seemed like forever, but ultimately I passed her inquisition and finally received the benefit of the doubt.

Twelve days later, I was released from the center on Thanksgiving Day.

Naomi's redemption took place in Bethlehem once she and Ruth returned there. Fairly quickly we learn in their story they rose from the famine and grief.

My redemption came slowly. *I* had taken too many pills. The doctor had not put the Xanax in my mouth. *I* had made the mistake. God forgave me. I knew that. But it took me ten years to forgive myself.

One night while studying at seminary, I got a phone call from my daughter. "Mom, are you watching '20/20'? Turn it on; they're talking about Xanax."

I did, and I cried. Ten years after I'd taken the stuff, I heard personal stories – testimony – about the addictive power of Xanax and how hard it is to stop. Ten years after my trial with those pills, with the help of a loving daughter and a television program, my redemption was complete.

God never abandoned me through that difficult time, just as God never abandoned Naomi. If in our crises she and I felt alone, it was our doing, not God's. God did not turn from her, even though she thought so. God did not turn from me either. We both received second chances. Where would any of us be without our Lord's amazing second chances?

Naomi had Ruth and Boaz and God. She called Boaz her kinsman-redeemer. I had my pastor, my God and my Jesus. Out of addiction, welcomed into their arms.

"O Jesus, blest Redeemer,
sent from the heart of God,
hold us who wait before Thee
near to the heart of God."

Thank you, redeeming God, for calling your children back to you over and over again.

QUESTIONS FOR LIFE:

1. What do you think of Naomi's story? Her feelings? Her behavior?

2. Have you ever felt desperate? Have you ever been bitter? Have you ever blamed God for any misfortunes in your life? Describe the situation(s).

3. Have you ever been drug-addicted? If so, for how long? Did you ever seek help, and from whom? What happened?

4. How did your addiction affect your family? Was there an intervention?

5. When you've made bad mistakes in your life, have you been able to admit them to yourself and others, forgive yourself and move on? Why? Why not?

"Be strong and courageous.
Do not be afraid or terrified...,
for the Lord your God goes with you;
he will never leave you nor forsake you."
Deuteronomy 31:6, NIV

Jael and Deborah
The Warriors

Was Jael brave or simply a woman who came up with a plot that worked? What if Sisera, the enemy commander, awakened before she could do the deed? Did she murder him or was her act justified by war?

The Israelites in those days had done evil in the sight of the Lord, "so the Lord sold them into the hands of Jabin, a king of Canaan," who cruelly oppressed them for twenty years. Sisera commanded Jabin's army. *Judges 4:2, NIV*

The people cried to the Lord for help.

Deborah, their leader and prophetess, called for Barak, her military general, and told him that God was commanding him into battle. Speaking God's words she said, "I will lure Sisera ... with his chariots and his troops to the Kishon River and give him into your hands."   *Judges 4:7, NIV*

Barak protested, saying he would go only if Deborah went with him. Deborah replied, "Very well, I will go with you. But because of the way you are going about this, the honor will not be yours, for the Lord will hand Sisera over to a woman."

Judges 4:9a, NIV

Events unfolded as Deborah said.

All of Sisera's troops perished in battle, but he "fled on foot to the tent of Jael, the wife of Heber the Kenite, because there were friendly relations between Jabin king of Hazor and the clan of Heber the Kenite."

Judges 4:17, NIV

Exhausted and believing he had found a safe hiding place, Sisera asked Jael for water; instead, she gave him milk. Then, when he fell asleep, she drove a tent peg "through his temple into the ground, and he died." *Judges 4:19-21, NIV*

Sisera perished at the hand of a woman who disagreed with her husband and acted on her own.

"You're brave! I couldn't do that!" more than one colleague said.

I'd resigned from a job after sixteen years to embark on a future unknown. I would have no income from work for I didn't know how long. All I knew that day as I said, "I've come to the end of the line," was that my future would be in Christian service. I didn't know I was headed to seminary to become a parish pastor.

Was I brave? Was I bold? At that time I didn't think so. In my mind I'd simply done what I had to do. The pieces fit. Divine nudges were leading me away from my newspaper job into a scary future, but I wasn't going alone. I had assurances from God, from Scripture, and from two relatives that I was making the right move.

Three years earlier I'd received my first call to ministry. I did not hear a voice, but two words sounded clear nonetheless – "prison ministry." I felt as if God had spoken. Immediately I thought, *God, you must be crazy! Me? I'm a parishioner in the pews!"* I wondered what God was planning.

Time passed and the "prison ministry" message receded to the back of my mind. A year and a half later it surfaced again, from my roommate at a church annual meeting. I'd registered late and didn't expect to share my room. She arrived late as well. She was a pastor who had presided at a funeral. When I found my belongings rearranged and hers on the other twin bed, I wondered how somebody else had obtained a key to *my* room?

That night she explained her lateness and told me about her ministry. My eyes grew misty. Of all the roommates I could have had, Sylvia had ministered in prisons.

Jump ahead almost two years. It's a Friday, the 13th. Work has been just dreadful. It's nearly 6 p.m., far later than I usually get home. I pull open my sliding porch door and hurl my keys. Good thing the piano was old!

I sink into my La-Z-Boy and begin a mental wrestle. I think of Jacob in the Old Testament doing battle with God, refusing to let go and seeking a blessing. *(Genesis 32:22-32)* Was I or wasn't I going to leave the job at the paper? Was I or wasn't I going to say yes to the signs I'd seen and the messages I'd heard? Was I or wasn't I going to surrender and let the Lord lead? Was I brave enough to do it?

Back and forth, back and forth. Stay at the paper or go? I draw a vertical line on paper and write "Reasons to Stay" on one side and "Reasons to Go" on the other. When I find the only "Reason to Stay" is weekly income, I know what I have to do. Only my decision still isn't easy.

I call my cousin, Debbie. Of all my extended family, she knows the Bible. She points me to *Jeremiah 29:11*, *John 10:14* and

John 10:27, verses that talk about God's plans for me and about how Jesus knows my name. I call my sister. She supports me from the secular point of view. I wrestle on.

Monday morning comes. I return to work. Today I must go in and tell my managing editor I'm resigning. Production details interfere. I have to wait 'til Tuesday. More details interfere then too. By now my heart is pounding. I can hardly concentrate. I leave work early and see my doctor. I'm wrought up and ask him to check my heart. He talks me down, calming me without a tranquilizer, even though I feel I need one. He assures me I'll be all right.

Wednesday morning. I'm finally able to see Deborah, my editor, and tell her, "I've come to the end of the line." We talk awhile and I sense a bit of awe from her, a bit of *I wish I could do something like that too.* And then she says as I refer to my expected future in Christian service, "I think the angels will support you." *Thank you, kind Deborah.*

Was I brave? Was I bold? Maybe. But mostly I did what I was led to do. I wrestled with God, and I knew if I'd said no, I wouldn't have been able to live with myself. How could I have faced the future?

I needn't have worried. God assured me with a push off the diving board: *You'll swim. I'll be with you all the way!*

Thank you, gracious God, for biblical calls to bravery, especially from Jesus who lovingly told us, "Do not let your hearts be troubled and do not be afraid."

John 14:27c, NIV

QUESTIONS FOR LIFE:

1. What do you think of Jael and her deed? Was she bold? Was she brave? Was her action justified by war? Why or why not?

2. What is your opinion of Deborah as a leader?

3. Have you ever thought you were brave? What was the situation?

4. Have you ever felt all your comfort zones collapsing? Why? What happened?

5. Have you ever left one job for another? Who and what helped you make your decision? What assurances did you receive that you were on the right course?

Let him kiss me with the kisses of his mouth –
  for your love is more delightful than wine.
Pleasing is the fragrance of your perfumes;
  your name is like perfume poured out.
No wonder the maidens love you!
Take me away with you – let us hurry!
Let the king bring me into his chambers.
                    Song of Songs 1:2-4, NIV

The Shulammite Woman
Solomon's Beloved

What's this? Erotic love poetry in the Bible? Yes, erotic love poetry in the Bible.

The Shulammite woman and her lover take delight in each other in *Song of Songs*. In intimate detail, they describe their longings and feelings for each other. They praise the physical beauty they see and use metaphorical language to describe parts of their bodies. "Your graceful legs are like jewels, the work of a craftsman's hands," the lover says as he gazes upon her.

Song of Songs 7:1b, NIV

The poem begins on their wedding day and then takes us back to their courtship and engagement. It includes a dream and ends expressing the power of love.

The poem may shock, and over the centuries its meaning has caused much debate. But overall it is a celebration – of physical love in marriage and the importance of sex in the world God created.

Song of Songs is a book of wisdom literature in the Old Testament.

I knew I loved Henry two years before I could tell him. Before that, the timing was not right. It was the longest wait of my life.

Finally the signs were in place. It was *"carpe diem"* – seize the day. I knew that if my courage failed, if I shied away and let the moment pass, it would not come again. Now or never!

I stewed over the chicken dinner (and

it wasn't stewed chicken!), wanting it to be just right. When Henry arrived and our evening began, I steered the conversation to past times at work and to updates on our adult children. I tried to keep my voice steady and my heartbeat under control. Finally it was almost time for him to leave.

"Henry," I said, with fear and trembling, "there's something I have to tell you. ... I love you. ... I've loved you for more than two years, from the time I left *The News*. I feel sheepish in telling you, but it's true, I love you."

He sat dumbfounded and silent for some time. I sat silent, too, nervously waiting for him to speak. At last he defended himself, saying he was flattered but protesting I did not know him. We had been colleagues at the newspaper for sixteen years, but he was right. I didn't totally know him. I admitted I didn't know *all* of him, but I added that if the parts of him I didn't know were as good a man as the parts I did know, it was enough.

I admitted my embarrassment, but I persisted, pointing out our similarities. We were both first-born children – he had a younger brother and I a younger sister. We were both "good kids" and good students. Our parents had been strict. We both played by the rules.

Then I went to my bookshelf and pulled off *When I Am An Old Woman I Shall Wear Purple*. I read him the poem about the woman in the purple dress with the red hat that didn't match, saying how much I loved the fact that woman dared to be herself, doing "wildish" things no matter what anyone thought. I said it was time for both of us to live, do something different, break out of the box, not flaunting any rules but enjoying the freedom that comes with age.

He sat and listened, then said a quick goodbye and left for the guest house where he was staying. I had thrown him the ball. I had said "my piece," and now I had to wait. I loved him but I knew from his restraint and silence he didn't love me. I didn't know whether he ever could or would.

About a month later, I received a call. Henry said, "We have to talk."

Hey, wait a minute! Isn't that what **the woman** *usually says?*

When I arrived, we talked in his upstairs living-room, face to face. He said, "Define your terms!" I asked him what he meant. "Do you mean permanent?" I answered yes, I meant permanent, as in life-long commitment and marriage.

He fell silent again, a long time. Finally, he said, "I can't go through it again." I knew he meant losing a wife. His Nancy had died less than three years before.

As I prepared to leave, Henry said he hoped I wasn't devastated. I said I wasn't, but I lied. I told him we'd been friends too long and I hoped we could remain so. He walked me to my car and we said goodnight under a full moon. It was the end of June. There was no hug, no kiss, no touch.

I ached and cried for two days. It felt like everything was lost. Back home in my apartment at seminary, I hugged my cat, tried to concentrate on my summer school class and listened over and over to Bette Midler sing *"The Rose."*

*"It's the heart afraid of breaking
that never learns to dance.
It's the dream afraid of waking
that never takes the chance."*

I did not blame him. In his position, I probably would have felt the same.

But it was not over. I had invited him to join me for the Fourth of July, and we had previously made plans to attend a writers' conference. Tuesday night that week in July, we processed the day and discussed what it felt like to have a story take on a life of itself. Emotion was high. Writing is "heady," evocative work.

It was time for me to leave. I thought our conversation was over, but three words stopped me. Henry rose from his seat, extended his arm, and said, "No, don't go!" – words I'd been longing to hear. I walked toward him. He enfolded me and kissed me. He took the chance. The romance began. We were engaged less than a month later.

Henry and I were married a year to the day after that chicken dinner. He has been and is my beloved. I love to tell him he's handsome. "Do you know how handsome you are?" "Have I told you before that I love you?"

He doesn't often say out loud he loves me, but I know he does. He writes it on notes, sometimes even on a reminder for an errand. He does kind deeds without a comment, waiting until I discover them and then grinning when I "fall all over him" with a "thank you." I *speak* the language of love; Henry *shows* it and writes it. It took me awhile to accept our different expressions of love.

Our life together has not been perfect. What marriage ever is? But Henry is my beloved, now and until death do us part.

"My lover is mine and I am his ..."
Song of Songs 2:16a, NIV

So far in this chapter that mentions erotic love poetry at the beginning, I have been sedate. So how's this for spice? Grannie's still gettin' it on at 69, and Grampie's still doin' IT at 77. Whoopee for senior sex! No condoms, no pill, no STDs (sexually transmitted diseases). Just us – just us, enjoying each other, because, so far, God has blessed us with good enough health. Our muscles and sinews and tendons and organs still work. Why shouldn't we enjoy them as long as we can?

The Bible tells us we're fearfully and wonderfully made. *(Psalm 139:14a, NIV)* Sex is a gift from God, not only for procreation but for pleasure and intimate communion. In today's world, sex has become perverted and sometimes ugly and horribly cruel, but God never meant it to be that way. Our bodies, the way we're made –

we're miracles of creation. We're meant to use our bodies rightly and give thanks every day that we can.

And if you think the lovin' need be over at 77, forget it. A charming couple I know just celebrated their 72nd wedding anniversary. They're both in their early 90s. They may not be doin' IT any more, but she can certainly still lean over and nibble his ear, and he can lift her chin and plant a good one on her lips. They can cuddle and hug and sit arm in arm, enjoying and loving each other. He plays the harmonica, and maybe he plays love songs for her, still and forever his bride, still and forever his one and only beloved.

Thank you, God of all creation, that erotic sexual love has a place in your world.

QUESTIONS FOR LIFE:

1. What do you think of *Song of Songs*? Are you shocked? Do you find the poem "over the top"? Why or why not?

2. If you are married, what's your relationship with your spouse? Do you speak the same language of love? Do you understand each other? Describe how you love one another.

3. Do you and your spouse take delight in each other? (That means, among other things, do you like sex?)

4. At this stage of your life, what is your body image? Are you comfortable in your own skin? How does *Song of Songs* have you feeling about your body?

5. *Song of Songs* is sometimes understood as the story of God's passionate love for God's people. How passionate is your relationship with God?

"But what about you?" [Jesus] asked.
"Who do you say I am?"
Simon Peter answered, "You are the Christ,
the Son of the living God."
Matthew 16:15-16, NIV

Martha
Confessor of the Faith

"Yes, Lord, ... I believe that you are the Christ, the Son of God, who was to come into the world."

John 11:27, NIV

With those words, Martha of Bethany, sister of Mary and Lazarus, answered Jesus, affirming that he was the resurrection and the life, as he had just told her he was.

Martha's brother, Lazarus, had died, and Martha said to Jesus, who had delayed arriving in Bethany even though he had heard Lazarus was sick, "Lord, if you had been here, my brother would not have died. But I know that even now God will give you whatever you ask." *John 11:21-22, NIV*

Jesus told her that her brother would rise again. Martha said she understood he would rise "in the resurrection at the last day." *John 11:24, NIV*

Then Jesus told her he was the resurrection and the life and that whoever believed in him would never die. He asked her if she believed it.

She said she did.

This exchange between Martha and Jesus takes place in the story of the death of Lazarus, narrated in Chapter 11 of the Gospel of John.

"Who was Jesus, and why did he die?"

The short question rather stunned me. Other questions had been longer. I did my best to answer quickly, as even more questioners were waiting. Like Martha, I said that Jesus was the Son of God. He was the

Incarnate One, the Savior of the world. I said he died to save people from their sins and bring salvation to all believers.

The look on my questioner's face indicated he seemed to be expecting more, but I sat silent. Finally, he nodded. I surmised that he was processing my answer and because he asked no follow-up question, I concluded that while he found my answer short, it was enough.

The situation was my "oral exam" before the Board of Ordained Ministry, a group of forty-six clergy charged with determining whether I was fit to join them as a preacher of the Word in The United Methodist Church.

Seven years had led up to the event.

In 1992 I served my local church as an alternate delegate to a larger church conference, the equivalent of a corporation's annual meeting. The majesty of organ, trumpets, choir and more than 1,000 people singing together thrilled me. The business sessions broadened my perspectives, showing me how the larger church handles different points of view. The service of ordination for new clergy opened my eyes to God's work in people's lives.

The candidates for ordination walked forward in white or black robes and knelt on benches arranged in a half-circle on the auditorium stage. The bishop and members of her cabinet approached each one and placed hands on heads or shoulders. The thought went through my mind, *You could be up there one day.*

The next year I attended the conference again. The last session before adjournment included a prayerful hymn, sung first in English, then in Spanish, and finally in Korean. Our new bishop, a man this time, left the stage and circulated among the people as the singing continued. Suddenly I felt a soft, gray gossamer veil descend upon my head down to my shoulders, then lift slowly and disappear. I took it as a sign, a mystical touch from heaven, and I wondered if it meant I was a step closer to a new life in ministry.

In 1994 I attended the large conference yet again – the Detroit Annual Conference of The United Methodist Church. I'd just left my job of sixteen years and was wondering about my future in the Christian service I'd told my newspaper managing editor I would be pursuing. It didn't take long to find out. At the end of the ordination service when the bishop invited people to come forward, people who felt they'd heard God's call to ministry, I rose and walked down the aisle, goose bumps on my arms and almost in tears. *All right, God, here I am. I think you're calling me to go to seminary.*

As the service ended and the congregation filed out, a member of that year's Board of Ordained Ministry talked with me for an hour, listening to my story, taking my contact information and understanding the signs I felt I'd been given to guide me on my way. *"Thank you, Rev. Tuttle."*

Later that month I applied to two seminaries and was accepted at both. I chose the one closer to home (with the prettier campus) and began school in late August.

For three years I studied at the Methodist Theological School in Delaware, Ohio, just north of Columbus. Telling you about seminary would take another book. I never had more homework. After eighteen years away from graduate school education, I didn't know whether I could "cut it," especially during that first term. But I did, and I graduated in May of 1997. Two-and-a-half weeks later, I was ordained as a probationary pastor, and two years after that I was fully ordained as an elder, having passed the requirements of that same Board of Ordained Ministry I've mentioned twice before.

My family attended the ordination celebration in the chapel at Adrian College. They saw Bishop Donald Ott place his hands on my head and tell me to "take authority as an elder" to preach the Word, teach and serve the people, and administer the church. My family and a large congregation of witnesses heard me confess my faith, committing myself to the ministry and service of my Lord and Savior Jesus, the Christ.

Thank you, O Most Holy God, for declarations of faith by which Christians affirm their belief in Father, Son and Holy Spirit.

QUESTIONS FOR LIFE:

1. Who is Jesus of Nazareth to you? Is he a good man, a great teacher? Why? Is he your Lord and Savior? Why or why not?

2. Have you ever been asked to confess your faith, not only in a creed, but in your own words and voice? When? Describe your feelings.

3. Have you ever felt God putting a special touch on your life, calling you to new service in your profession, your home, or your church? When? How? What happened? Describe the situation.

Yea, though I walk through
the valley of the shadow of death,
I will fear no evil: for thou art with me ...
Psalm 23:4a, KJV

Mary, Mother of Jesus
Watching a Loved One Die

She was there at the foot of the cross. "Woman, here is your son," Jesus said.

John 19:26, NRSV

How could she have watched him? How could she have stood to see his agony? How could Mary have borne such piercing pain?

Perhaps she remembered the words old Simeon had spoken when Jesus was eight days old. "This child is destined to cause the falling and rising of many in Israel, and to be a sign that will be spoken against, so that the thoughts of many hearts will be revealed.

And a sword will pierce your own soul too."

Luke 2:34-35, NIV

Her soul must have been seared. Her heart must have been broken.

That day we call Good Friday, Mary of Nazareth watched her child die.

Death came for my mother on Friday, Nov. 15, 2002. I had seen other people die, the last breath taken, the monitor flatlining. I had been present with families at that final moment and united with them in prayer. With my mother, I was the only family member in the room. Her overnight nurse was the only other person at her bedside.

Mom's weight had fallen to less than 100 pounds. Her arms hung at her sides. The skin of her face stretched over cheekbones that protruded, and her teeth appeared larger than ever before. Her thin skin was translucent, shining, ethereal. I thought about Moses' shining face as he descended from Mount Sinai. *(Exodus 34:29-35)* My mother's face was beautiful in death.

I had not considered her beautiful in life. She was always attractive, even pretty, but not beautiful. In death, radiance appeared. Looking at her, before her final breaths and her life ebbed away, I felt the presence of God. Death, at that moment, was holy, every bit as holy as birth. It was the completion – the cycle of life.

I did not keep a bedside vigil the night before Mom died. I knew I'd be alone after she was taken away. There would be much to do to get the house ready for relatives arriving for the memorial service, so I had a good night's sleep in the bedroom next to hers and was rested on Friday morning.

Watching my mother's last few breaths, lying on the bed beside her, I brushed a strand of hair back off her forehead. And I said, plaintively, "Oh Mama, we're loving you into paradise." I had not called my mother "mama" since I was a child. I had never thought of her as "mama" all those years. Now, at 59, I was calling my 88-year-old mother "mama." Does death, somehow, take us back to our beginnings? I cried for awhile after her final breath, but not with overwhelming grief. Mom's death had been expected. I had pre-grieved in some ways for more than two years.

She had suffered a heart attack just days before her birthday in August of 2000. The doctors said, "You need six bypasses." She refused. I wanted her to have the surgery, but terror overtook her. She had never been cut open or stitched up in her life. (She needed cataract surgery too, but she turned that down as well.)

Given her heart decision, her team of cardiologists worked to keep her alive. They juggled pills in a cocktail of medications, focusing on potassium. They monitored her carefully and took her driver's license away. She made a pretty good recovery and did well through 2001.

Pneumonia in January 2002 began the nearly year-long downhill spiral. Her strength was ebbing away. In August, on her 88th birthday, she asked me, "Am I dying?" I took a long time answering at that luncheon table, watching her pick haphazardly at her food. Finally and quietly, as gently as I could, I said, "Yes, maybe you are. They say that appetite is one of the first things to go."

She lost weight as summer rolled to fall, but her spirit remained intact. Friends came to visit. Home health aides met her needs. Ten days before she died I received a call. Aides had found blood at her bedside. I rushed the 100 miles to East Lansing. One look and I said, "We've got to get you to the hospital." She argued but not forcefully. A 911 call brought the paramedics who carried my mother in a sheet, hammock-like, down the hallway in her home because the gurney would not fit. She was easy to lift.

She spent three days in the hospital. Her doctor mentioned a transfusion but she would have none of it. She wanted to be home to die in the bed she had shared with my father for 39 years.

A week to the day before her death, we carried her home. I stayed with her as long as I could before returning to my pastoral duties over the weekend. We hired around-the-clock nurses and called in Hospice. Mom would be well-cared for until I could return, and morphine would be administered. I tried to leave by 6:30, fully dark in Michigan in November. But Mom needed to talk. Emphatically she told me, "I'm going to die tonight. I'm ready. I'm ready for God to take me. I'm going to die tonight."

Her animated comments made me chuckle inside. I didn't tell her, but I knew she'd be alive the next day and likely the day after that. I knew, but she seemed not to know, that her life force would have to weaken some more, that she would have to lose her speech and enter that final coma. I knew that her death would be on God's timetable, not her own.

What I did say that Friday evening was, "No, I don't think you'll die tonight."

She didn't. On Monday of her final week, her aide told me she was sitting up in bed, arms fully extended, railing at God, "Why won't you take me? Why won't you take me? I'm ready to go." Tuesday night I called her. She was difficult to understand. Her words were garbled. She sounded exhausted. The conversation was short. I told her I loved her. It was the last time we talked.

Sometime during Mom's final days, a former aide named Jessica came to pay a call. Mom had mentioned Jessica more than once. The beautiful young woman arrived with a card in her hand, and was ushered back to my mother's bedroom. She sat on the edge of Mom's bed. I stood nearby and watched. The looks on the faces of those two women brought tears to my eyes. Clearly they loved each other. An 88-year-old dying woman was looking into the shining face of a twenty-something. Love bridged the spectrum of years. At that moment I finally knew why my cousins had called my mother Auntie Mame. Even with death drawing near, my mother had a spirit that soared!

God gave me the gift of watching my mother die. You may wonder how I can say that. But I saw her death as the omega, the final chapter and act. God was in the bedroom with my mother, her aide and me. God gave my mother life at birth. She had new life with God in death.

Thank you, God of the ages, for my mother and her life of 88 years.

QUESTIONS FOR LIFE:

1. Have you ever, like Jesus' mother and me, watched a loved one die? What did you observe? How did the experience affect you? What did you learn?

2 . With all the ways that death can come to human beings, with all the agony and heartbreak there can be, what do you feel about death? Does it frighten you?

3. Do you believe in eternal life? Why or why not? What have you been taught about it?

4. If we know that our loved ones have died to eternal life, how does that affect the way we grieve?

There is a time for everything,
and a season for every activity under heaven...
Ecclesiastes 3:1, NIV

Esther, the Queen
For Such a Time as This

She was a queen. She was in the right place at the right time to save her people.

Esther became Queen of Persia after the former queen was banished for disobedience. The beautiful young Esther, a Jew, pleased King Xerxes and he chose her from his royal harem. She and her people were his subjects because 100 years earlier the Jews had been deported from Judah during the Babylonian captivity.

Esther's older cousin, Mordecai, became a government official for the king and foiled an assassination plot. He refused, however, to bow down to the king's second-in-command, Haman, who bristled, plotting to destroy him and the Jewish people. Haman tricked the king, persuading him to issue a Jewish death sentence. When Mordecai learned of the edict, he informed Esther and urged her to "go into the king's presence to beg for mercy and plead with him for her people." *Esther 4:8b, NIV*

But to see the king, a person had to be summoned, and Esther had not been summoned for thirty days. Mordecai replied: "Do not think that because you are in the king's house you alone of all the Jews will escape. For if you remain silent at this time, relief and deliverance for the Jews will arise from another place, but you and your father's family will perish. And who knows but that you have come to royal position for such a time as this?" *Esther 4:13-14, NIV*

Esther then replied: "Go, gather together all the Jews who are in Susa, and fast for me. ... I and my maids will fast as you do. When this is done, I will go to the king, even though it is against the law. And if

I perish, I perish." *Esther 4:16, NIV*

Esther did not perish. Haman's vengeance against Mordecai did not succeed, and he, not the Jews, met death. Xerxes heeded Esther's pleas for her people. She, indeed, served as Queen of Persia "... for such a time as this."

All this and more of the story is told in ten chapters in the Old Testament book that bears Esther's name.

For such a time as this, fall season 2011, I am a recovering co-dependent. What that means for me (co-dependency can affect each person differently) is that I am learning better ways of relating to alcoholic people and taking care of myself. Alcoholism is a family disease. Everyone close to an alcoholic is affected. I expect many of you know this from your own experience.

Alcoholism affected me early. My mother did not drink heavily when I was a child. I don't remember her over-drinking until I was in college. But I grew up with Mom dictating family life, imposing her will on us and cottoning few differences of opinion. As the years went by, her drinking escalated, as I have referenced in preceding chapters. A counselor, actually, told me I had grown up in an alcoholic home. Co-dependency became my way of coping. Now, late in life though it is, I am learning not to cope, not to be the "fix it" person, but to live.

I know I don't have to tell you this. I could very well keep the information private. But I also know what I wrote in this book's introduction about bravery and about encouraging you to take risks and venture in new directions as you feel the power of the Spirit. If I can't or won't take my own advice, what kind of person am I? If I am a person of integrity, a woman who tells the truth so the world might split open (see the Muriel Rukeyser quote on the frontispiece), I need to walk the walk, not just put pretty words on paper.

More than a year ago, when I first wrote this chapter, it was very different. At that time, which I also saw as "for such a time as this," I felt my relationship with my mother had been redeemed. I was looking for redemption; I wanted it. And, with God's help, I achieved it, to the extent that I was able to replace negative words with positives – "cruel, controlling, critical" became "classy, colorful, creative." My load had been lifted. I felt free from the past. I thought the freedom was permanent, but it was not. Continuing work on family of origin issues in the co-dependency recovery process brought old memories back to life.

Now I am seeking redemption in the mother relationship again. It saddens me that I need to retrace steps, but I know the ones I took earlier were not in vain. They laid the foundation for current growth – in counseling once more. Discovering my co-dependency was a huge blow to my self-esteem, a step back in the sand, but regaining redemption should come faster because of what has come before. Redemption in other relationships should come faster too. It is happening in one that had been very difficult recently. I am grateful.

In God's world, time is not "khronos" but "kairos." Time follows no clock. It is always right. Things happen for a reason. (How many times have we heard that?) Life is agony. Life is ecstasy. They are clichés, but clichés for a reason. They are true.

Now, I would share my favorite Bible verses. They have guided me and comforted me for years, and while sometimes I have doubted them and railed against them and God in pain and agony, nevertheless they have stood. That is what the Word of God does. It stands forever, a bulwark against anything life can throw our way.

The Word of God stands *for such a time as this.*

"For I know the plans I have for you, says the Lord. They are plans for good and not for evil, to give you a future and a hope."
Jeremiah 29:11, TLB

"Trust in the Lord with all your heart, and lean not on your own understanding. In all your ways acknowledge Him, and He shall direct your paths."

Proverbs 3:5-6, NKJV

Thank you, Almighty God.
Amen, and amen.

QUESTIONS FOR LIFE:

1. What does "for such a time as this" mean to you? Have you ever experienced such a time? Describe the situation.

2. Are any of your relationships problematic? Why?

3. Do you have any unresolved issues with people close to you? What can you do about them? What do you want the other person to do? Are reconciliation and redemption possible any time soon? How? How can you take the first step?

4. Do you see Jesus as your redeemer? Why or why not?

5. What factors make it possible for redemption to take place?

Appendix A
User's Guide – Individual

- 1. Go to a favorite place in your home or other comfortable location where you can be alone for 30-45 minutes. Make the room a sanctuary in any way you wish.
- 2. Begin with prayer. Ask the Holy Spirit to open your mind and heart to each story in the Bible and in this book. Have a pen or pencil and notebook on hand.
- 3. On your first day, review the Contents of this book and read the Introduction. Get a feel for what you will encounter.
- 4. Day 2 and thereafter, read the introductory part of each chapter and then the Bible passage. Ask yourself how you and

this woman are alike. Are there ways in which you are different? What does she have you remembering about your own life? Do you see her the way she's introduced in the chapter, or do you have another point of view?

For example, *were* Mary and Martha sibling rivals as mentioned in the chapter about sisters, or is that too much of a stretch? *Were* Mary Magdalene and the other women a support group as mentioned in the chapter called "Followers of Jesus"?

● 5. Return to *She and You and Me* and read my story in the chapter and then the questions for life. Answer them in your head or in your notebook, if you wish.

● 6. Journal your reactions as you feel led to; write or ponder anything the chapter and the Bible stories bring to mind. Think about your life as a teacher or musician, a mother or sister, and perhaps begin writing your own story.

● 7. End your time with prayer. Be enriched and blessed.

● 8. Since there are twenty-one chapters in *She and You and Me*, plan on three weeks for this study if you can devote 30-45 minutes a day. Otherwise, set aside two or three days a week, for seven or ten-eleven weeks.

    ● 9. Share what you wish to share with loved ones, or ponder your experience in your heart.

Appendix B
User's Guide - Group

The guidelines presented here are designed for use in homes, senior citizen and community centers, spirituality and retreat centers as well as houses of worship. They can apply equally in ecumenical and denominational settings.

Newcomers to Bible study are especially encouraged to participate in this exploration, to become acquainted with Scripture through the stories of women whose lives can intersect with their own. Hopefully newcomers will find that they and the Bible women have much in common and will enjoy studying the Bible enough to move on to other "books" and stories. The questions at the end of the chapters are "practical living" for the most part rather than deeply theological, offering a "user-friendly" introduction to the Bible.

As for "seasoned" Bible students, they are invited to become better acquainted with the featured Bible women in this unique Scripture-memoir format. Everyone is invited to reflect, pray, and perhaps then write, sculpt, paint – use whatever creative talent – to share parts of a personal journey.

As the leader/facilitator for group study of *She and You and Me*:

- 1. Plan sessions of 75-90 minutes for five or six weeks to twenty-two weeks straight through. The shorter periods of time, quarterly, would allow all the chapters to be completed in a year, if that is a goal for your group.

- 2. Arrange tables in a rectangle or place round tables close together so participants can see each other and have a place to set this book, a Bible, a beverage and snack (if desired). Make the setting comfortable and informal.

• 3. Begin each session with prayer. Invite the Holy Spirit to open each person's mind and heart.

• 4. For Session 1 – Make name tags and introductions (if participants don't know each other from previous associations). Be invitational. The aim is exploration and enjoyment, like a Bible safari. Growth and sharing are goals. New points of view may be considered, but there are no right or wrong answers or interpretations. Learn from one another and have fun.

Review the Contents of this book. Read the Introduction and discuss it. Get a feel for what you will encounter.

Ask the group to read Chapter 1 *Mary, Mother of Jesus,* the Bible verses about her and the chapter-ending questions in preparation for the next session.

End the time with prayer. Be enriched and blessed.

• 5. For Sessions 2-22 – After opening with prayer, review the introduction to the "the woman of the day" in *She and You and Me.* Read the suggested Bible verses about her. Get to know her. In many cases my chapter introductions focus on one aspect of the woman's life and on selected verses, presenting "my take."

For example, I feature Miriam as a singer/musician, but she was a dancer, a prophetess and a leprosy sufferer too. So round out the picture, especially if other "takes" are different from mine. Read all the Bible has to offer about each specific woman. Again, take the time to really get to know her.

Discuss how you and the participants and the Bible woman are alike. Ask yourselves how are you different. Share stories, feelings, insights, memories – as you wish – guided by the queries in "Questions for Life." (Feel free, always, to expand with more questions.)

End with prayer. "Assign" Chapter 2 (or whatever chapter you choose) as "homework" for next week. Follow the same pattern each time you meet.

As you are guiding your group, please do not focus on the "my story" part of each chapter during your time together. Have everyone read it at home, on their own time. I've simply presented it as an example of sharing my life and of "finding ourselves in the Bible."

If as leader/facilitator you feel a chapter might not produce much discussion, use more than one chapter at a time. But, again, get to know each Bible woman as much as possible and make her story your own.

The chapters do not necessarily have to be used in order, except perhaps for *Sarah, Michal* and *Abigail*, which are about my mother and me and build to some extent upon each other. Also, three earlier chapters – *Miriam, Dorcas* and *Priscilla* – introduce the musician, seamstress and teacher aspects of my mother's (and my) life and are lead-in chapters to *Sarah, Michal* and *Abigail*.

Acknowledgments

Much help and many "booster shots" propelled me along the way. Without those who provided them, this book wouldn't be in print. So thank you, with a grateful heart:

Penny W. – earliest encourager

Melva – early chapter/ manuscript reader

Jane and Nancy – chapter reviewers

Penny P. – group Bible study advocate, first draft "endurer"

Patsy – early chapter and manuscript reader, information provider (about your mother), kind letter correspondent

Becky – manuscript reader, publication encourager

Debbie – photo, question and suggestion provider, manuscript reader, emailer

Karla and Marlis – photo and comment providers (about your grandmother)

Green Lake Conference Center, Green Lake, WI – provider of serenity and beauty where I felt God's closeness, heard God's voice, and received invaluable help with writing

Julie – writing "teacher," prayer and Scripture suggestion provider, manuscript reader, encourager extraordinaire

Sharon – manuscript reader, suggestion provider

Joan and Mary Fran, Sisters, IHM – manuscript readers, Bible study facilitators

Tracie – manuscript reader, Bible study hostess

Debi and Jackie – clergy sister manuscript readers

Pam – final manuscript reader

Lane and Charlie – self-publishing information and suggestion providers

Kathy – professional manuscript editor

Linda – cover designer

Heather and Sandy – print production professionals

Ben – photo consultant

Marcia – manuscript reader, provider of love, the daughter who always "has my back"

Henry – "computerer," home editor, formatter, provider of love, patience, everything

About the Author

Margaret Passenger is a woman of three careers –
high school English teaching,
newspaper copy editing,
ordained ministry in The United Methodist Church.
She has a passion for sharing Scripture and has led Bible studies for more than fifteen years.
Now, in retirement, she is engaged in another life adventure – as a writer.
She and her husband, Henry, live in southeast Michigan.
Email address: revmarg@gmail.com